IS THAT YOUR VOICE, LORD?

Eight Christians tell how to discover God's will

IS THAT YOUR VOICE, LORD?

Edited by Geoffrey Grogan

Eight Christians tell how
to discover God's will

The insights of
Donald Bridge,
Lorimer Gray,
Neil Innes,
Pauline Stableford,
Paul Harvey,
Mary Mealyea,
Joel Edwards,
Maizie Smith

Christian Focus Publications

© 1995 Christian Focus Publications
ISBN 1–85792–119–4

Published by
Christian Focus Publications Ltd
Geanies House, Fearn, Ross-shire,
IV20 1TW, Scotland, Great Britain.

Cover design by Donna Macleod

Printed and bound in Great Britain by
Cox & Wyman Ltd., Reading, Berkshire

CONTENTS

Geoffrey Grogan

Geoff was born in 1925 and, although English, has lived more than half his life in Glasgow. He and Eva his wife have three grown-up children. He lectured for 35 years at the Glasgow Bible College (formerly known as BTI), for the last 21 as principal. He also taught for 4 years at the London Bible College and as a visitor in Bulgaria, Hungary and the USA. He has written a number of books, and since retiring in 1990 he has concentrated on writing, but is also part-time minister of Shotts Baptist Church in Lanarkshire. His interests include overseas mission, music, art, architecture, history, philosophy and literature—and people!

Donald Bridge

Don is sixty-three and lives in the city of Durham. He is married to Rita: they have two sons and six grandchildren. He is a Baptist minister, now seconded to mission work and leadership consultancy with The Evangelization Society. He has pastored three churches and 'planted' several others. Since 1972 he has also written or co-authored fifteen books of popular theology, and made numerous contributions to Scripture Union Bible notes. His spare time interests include walking, sailing, archaeology, reading and stamp collecting. His church membership is currently with Bethany Church in Houghton-le-Spring, near Durham.

Lorimer Gray

Lorimer grew up in the southside of Glasgow, lived in Edinburgh and Reading before travelling north to settle in Nethybridge. He is married to Moira, they have two daughters and a son and, as a family, worship in the local church in Nethybridge.

Neil Innes

Neil was born and brought up in Ross-shire. On leaving school, he worked on the Hydro Electric Schemes in Wester Ross. In 1956, he joined the regular Army and served nine years in the Royal Army Medical Corps. During which period, he qualified as a State Registered Nurse.

On leaving the regular Army in 1965 Neil became a full-time Scripture Reader with the Soldiers' and Airmen's Scripture Readers Association. In 1977 he became the Area Representative for Scotland, Northern Border Counties of England and the Isle of Man.

He and his wife Barbara have four grown-up children. They live in Balerno, Midlothian and attend Bellevue Evangelical Church, Edinburgh.

Pauline Stapleford

Pauline was born in 1938 in Sale, Cheshire. She has a BA in German and French from Nottingham University as well as a BTI Diploma, RSA TEFL certificate. Pauline taught English in Finland before spending 18 years with European Christian Mission doing extension work in Scandinavia, office work and then as church pastoral assistant in Germany. Then she taught English and did office work for four years in the Far East. Her present ministry is in Hungary teaching at a Bible Institute and church planting work amongst the migrant Chinese population.

Mary Mealyea

Mary, known as Ray to her friends, graduated at Dundee University in 1976 as a doctor. Married to Harry, they have four children. Harry is minister of Bargeddie Parish Church, on the outskirts of Glasgow. Harry and Mary served the Lord as missionaries in Iran and Pakistan before returning to Scotland. During the 1980s, Mary was Director of CARE Scotland. She has written two books, *Free From The Past* and *A Child At Any Cost*.

Paul Harvey

Born in 1946, Paul has been in secular employment all of his adult life. He became a Christian in 1975 through the witness of a colleague at work, and has always felt that the Lord requires him to remain in industry as 'salt' and 'light' in the workplace. Despite painful events in Paul's private life, the Lord has proved faithful and given him many opportunities of service. Those whom the Lord has not called into full-time Christian ministry will identify with Paul's story.

Joel Edwards

Joel is a leading figure within the evangelical church in the UK, holding senior positions within black and white church traditions.

He is currently UK Development Director at the Evangelical Alliance UK, which represents a million churchgoers from a dozen denominations. Encouraging Christian co-operation across denominational and cultural lines is one of his tasks. Joel, who is married with two children, is also the pastor of the New Testament Church of God in London's East End.

Three years spent at London Bible College gaining a

degree in theology were followed by 10 years in the Inner Probation Service, two of them at Holloway Prison for women. He reflects: 'My time as a Probation Officer convinced me of Christianity's relevance as a message of hope for human beings.'

A former General Secretary of the African Caribbean Evangelical Alliance, Joel remains on its council and also serves on the national executive of the New Testament Church of God, one of the UK's largest black denominations.

Joel was born in Kingston, Jamaica, and came to Britain in 1960 at the age of eight.

Maizie Smyth

A missionary with UFM WORLDWIDE since 1976, Maizie is working at present in Kisangani, Haut Zaire. She previously trained as a secretary and worked in local government before Bible School training at the BTI in Glasgow. Her main ministry is Bible School teaching and finance, although as the only missionary there at present, a lot of time is spent 'listening'. The close knit family, church and community life during her childhood near Broughshane, Ballymena, has well equipped her for rural village work in Zaire.

WHAT THIS BOOK IS ABOUT

Geoffrey Grogan

There was once a boy who had a strange experience during the night.

He heard a voice calling to him. He was puzzled by it. Whose voice was it? He ran to the old priest who was asleep not far away. 'Here I am; you called me,' he said. But the priest denied this and sent him back to bed. Again the voice came; again the old man told him to take his rest. But the voice persisted and addressed him a third time. This time Eli took it with due seriousness and said to Samuel, 'If he calls you, say, "Speak, Lord, for your servant is listening."' You can read the whole story in 1 Samuel 3.

A modern-day Christian may find himself in a somewhat similar situation to Samuel in that Old Testament story. He is aware of a voice calling him. It may be that a brother or sister in the Lord has suggested a move in some new direction. On the other hand, there may be no voice audible with the physical ear, but he is aware of a special stirring in his heart. Perhaps events are happening in which he thinks he discerns a voice calling him to make some major change in his life.

A voice is speaking, but is it the voice of God?

It is to be hoped that such a modern Samuel has an Eli to consult. A pastor has an important place in such situations and a Christian would be unwise not to recognize this. This book is certainly not designed to be a substitute for godly advice from a man or woman's pastor. Sometimes such a pastoral adviser might appreciate having a book which can be made available in such a situation.

Here eight Christians tell their stories. They are most varied characters, in background, in temperament, in the shape life has taken, even in some ways in theology, although they all accept the supreme authority of the Bible. They are also extremely varied in the kinds of work they do in the service of Christ.

None of them claims infallibility. In fact they freely admit they have made mistakes. They are however united by the fact that each has sought God's guidance and also in the conviction that he has given it to them.

The term 'full-time service' is often used to describe the work of certain Christians as distinct from others. Some years ago, the writer of this Introduction was involved in a discussion with two other men, one old enough to be his father, the other young enough to be his son. He used the term 'full-time Christian service'. The older man reacted somewhat sharply. 'I spent my whole working life in a bank. I did all my work there as an offering to my Saviour. Tell me, was I in full-time Christian service or was I not?'

The point was well made, and well taken. The expression is not a very happy one.

It is quite true that there are forms of Christian service which have the communication of Christian truth in evangelism or in the teaching and care of Christians as their main feature. Christians guided into this kind of service are often aware of the fact that it is a call from God to a lifetime of specialised service and pastoral responsibility. This does not however invalidate my friend's insight.

For the Christian, all life is Divine vocation. The call of God is of a most radical kind for all of us, for it is, first and foremost, a call to come to Christ, to respond to him in faith. This leads to a reorientation of life under the sovereignty of God. If a call to specific service comes subsequent to that gracious invitation, this is a further unfolding of the purpose of God for that Christian's life.

Most of us have no difficulty, at least in general terms, with the idea that God's intention for us is that we should spend our lives in the service of Christ. After all, he has done so much for us in his agonizing death on the cross, that we want to bring our service as a love-gift to him.

The real problems come when we begin to think about specifics. These problems are not only connected with specialised service, such as a possible call to be a pastor or a missionary and so to train for such ministry. There are also such vital questions as who I should marry or whether I should marry at all. What kind of job does God intend I should do?

There are other issues too on which I need to be aware of God's guidance. They may not seem so big but they all affect the shape my life will take. There is the question of a possible response by me to the need for another teacher in the Sunday school. To which of the many charities that clamour for my attention should I give money? Can I help to do something about the unemployed people in my community, and, if so, what?

Questions, questions, questions. But how can I get answers? How can I know what God wants me to do? 'Is that YOUR voice, Lord?'

We hope the stories in this book will help you. Read them. They are about people who wrestled with such questions. They do not give slick, easy answers, because none of them has found that the Christian life can be reduced to a formula or even to a set of formulae. They are able nevertheless to thank God that he has not failed them, and that, in many different ways, he has made known what he wanted them to do.

You may feel more at home with some of them than with others. Because they are such different people and come from such varied backgrounds this is inevitable. At times you may find that you would have responded differently in a given situation or understood the significance of a particular event—or even a Scripture—in a different way. Obviously you will not want to treat them as infallible examples but as fellow-Christians from whom you may learn, as you prayerfully reflect on their stories in the light that comes from God's word.

You see, there has been no attempt at uniformity, no move to press them all into the same mould. Each person has told the story with sincerity and honesty in his or her own way. Because of this, you may well find that you learn something different from each one.

Another point needs to be made about how to use this volume. Please start at the beginning and go on to the end. You see, some people have a funny way of reading a book. They go to the last chapter of it almost immediately!

If it's fiction, they want to see how it all ends, even

though that probably makes little sense until they have seen how the story unfolds. If it's non-fiction, they hope the author has given all his main conclusions in the final chapter. Perhaps if they read that, they need not spend time reading the rest of the book at all!

The stories these eight people tell are followed by a final chapter in which an attempt is made to set out some Biblical principles. Do resist the temptation to go straight there. That chapter is not intended to stand on its own and its references to the stories told by these people will be meaningless unless you have read through the book.

That chapter aims to set out, clearly and with reasonable brevity, principles of God's guidance and calling to be found within the pages of Scripture, but the purpose of the chapter, as of the entire book, is practical. We need to be able to see that these principles really work in the lives of ordinary flesh and blood Christians, and it is better to read their stories first.

After all, this is what happens in the Bible itself. With the exception of those sections of the Pentateuch (the Five Books of Moses) that are about the Mosaic Law, there is a preponderance of stories in the earlier books in each Testament, such as Genesis and parts of Exodus and Numbers in the Old Testament and the four Gospels and the Acts of the Apostles in the New, while there is a preponderance of principles in the later books, such as the prophets and the letters of Paul.

As you read, pray. Seek an understanding of God's will for your own life—and may God give you light!

1

HAVE BIBLE, WILL TRAVEL

Donald Bridge

'Your husband had an accident at work. But there's nothing to worry about: he's got three doctors and four nurses seeing to him.'

These absurd words of intended re-assurance, addressed to my mother by a cloth-capped workman on the doorstep, are the earliest words I can recollect. My father was an instrument charge-hand in the vast chemical factory which stretched along the north bank of the river Tees in county Durham, in the north of England. When the wind blew from the north over Stockton it carried the sour smell of ammonia: when it blew from the south we smelled the rotten-eggs odour of hydrogen-sulphide from the smoke of the steel-furnaces.

I was four years old, and the year was 1935. Earliest memories are said to provide a significant clue to character and personality. Perhaps that overheard conversation (and the hurried bus-ride to the hospital that followed) contributed to the profound sense of irrational insecurity which dominated my shy, asthmatic and rather gloomy childhood. Perhaps the awareness of the grim years of recession, poverty and unemployment took their toll too.

Yet there was nothing repressive or perfectionist about family life for me and my little sister. Both parents were devout, tolerant, cheerful members of the Christian Brethren. Mother was a product of that movement and, as she often said, could never recall a time when she did not love Jesus. Dad was quite different, a product of a tough, unbelieving, left-wing family whose philosophy was socialism and whose pleasures were drinking and gambling. He had been suddenly converted to faith in Christ through 'accidentally' entering the wrong building on his way to a political meeting. He heard the gospel once, believed immediately, and gave his public testimony in an open-air meeting the same night. This all happened before I was born: to me evangelical Christianity was simply the way to live and believe. My parents were two of the most consistent and lovable Christians I have ever known, and our local church throbbed with life and love.

Father himself was a gifted lay-preacher with a mind soaked in scripture. He had a remarkable way of thinking in pictures. His homespun analogies were brilliant, and he related his talks to real life much more effectively than most preachers. I travelled with him wherever he preached, preferring him to any other speaker.

In my introspection and oddly-felt unhappiness I became an avid reader. My indiscriminate hunt through hundreds of books taught me the magic of words, whether they came from Moses, John Buchan, Richmal Crompton, the apostle John, or Arthur Ransome! Sometimes it occurred to me that I would like to spin words myself, but never that I would be a public speaker.

DONALD BRIDGE

A war lost and won
In early teens I tried to give up God. The family moved
from Stockton, and found themselves in a short-lived
church-plant whose members were singularly unattrac-
tive. This church was marked by bigotry, narrow vision,
bickering, and the complacent smugness of people convinced that they alone in town had the Truth. I concluded
the opposite. My parents' faith, I decided, was so superior to theirs, it must represent some unattainable
super-religion. And if what I saw in church was the
normal, then that wasn't worth having. One was
unreachable, the other undesirable. With all the stub-
bornness of an introvert, I dug in my heels, refused to
attend worship, and stopped saying my prayers.

In short—as a world war staggered towards its awful
conclusion, a personal war began in my heart. It lasted
less than a year. Some elementary astronomy appalled
me with its picture of an empty universe. Stirrings of
sexual awareness disturbed me with their potential for
new misbehaviour. Scriptures unconsciously learned in
childhood pursued me. One snowy January evening I
slipped into the Gospel Hall again, to hear a visiting
Open Air Mission evangelist. His words were so personal that I suspected him of being primed by my parents.
Then second thoughts prevailed, and I recognized the
call of God. I found, mysteriously, that I wanted to be a
Christian. How it happened, and precisely when, I could
not say.

I was rather like a man on a walking tour who crosses
between two adjoining countries at some point where the
border is not marked. A while ago he was in one country,
and a little later he is quite certainly in another, recognis-

able by the changing landscape. But precisely when and how he has crossed the border he is not sure. When I was thirteen I still lived in one country of the soul. Two years later I was well across the border, and the views were different. I could be no clearer than that. So I asked for baptism.

It was this visible step, plus my discovery (in long talks with my father) of the grace of God, that most clearly committed me to an open Christian profession. The message of the cross astonished me. For *me*? Complete forgiveness and a new standing with God? The meaning of the atonement became astonishingly clear; its cost to Christ devastating; its total unmerited gift to me enrapturing.

Two ambitions now motivated me. I wanted other people to know Jesus. And I wanted to get a real grip on the Bible. The little church had now closed. We moved to a happier version in Redcar, and then back to Hebron Church in Stockton, where it had all begun in the 1930's. It was a place to which you could invite friends, schoolmates, workmates, and see some of them converted. I recall writing in my diary one December, 'This year seventy people have become Christians at Hebron, and Rita and I have been directly connected with forty of them.' (Rita was the doctor's receptionist just down the road from the foundry where I now worked as a metallurgist. We seemed to bump into each other surprisingly often. Unknown to us, we were hot tips for the next Hebron wedding—as so we proved to be.)

Church and study

The Christian Brethren did two immensely enriching things for me. They stimulated my appetite for the Bible, and they encouraged me to explore my gifts and my role in church life.

The movement has always set its face against the idea of professional clergy (except as foreign missionaries). For the continuing leadership of their church life they depend on a succession of their own young men growing in the faith, taking on responsibility, and in turn handing on the torch, as lay-elders, teachers, leaders and preachers.

The idea was based on Paul's word to Timothy, often quoted in the Authorised Version which was our only translation in those days: 'The things that thou hast heard of me ... commit thou to faithful men who shall be able to teach others also' (2 Timothy 2:2).

Our leaders took this seriously, and so did several of us. I set myself a ten-year study course, from Genesis to Revelation, requiring about two hours per day, and using commentaries and handbooks with the text. I purposely widened my reading to largely non-Brethren writers. So I discovered, for example, Archbishop Trench on the Parables and Miracles (complete with quotations from Church Fathers).

My principal guide was *Explore The Book*, a six-volume introduction to the whole Bible written by the Baptist, Sidlow Baxter. Another treasure was *The Expositor's Bible*, a sixty-volume set which I discovered on a second-hand shelf, and arranged to buy one volume per week at a shilling a piece (after a few weeks the shopkeeper took me on trust and let me take the lot home).

Most central of all to my self-imposed task was a loose-leaf Bible with broad margins and room for blank pages to be interleaved. In this I made my own notes as I went along, in tiny Indian-ink script. I still have it, battered and worn. I smile now to re-read the notes and trace my developing understanding from Dispensationalism through to a mild Calvinism. What all this gave me was a possession priceless beyond measure: an overview of the Word as God had given it, book by book, narrative, poetry, law, anecdote, prophecy, apocalypse, gospel and epistle. Slowly my life became dominated by the sense of calling to know and to make known these riches.

Introducing Christ
Parallel to this, the ambition developed to share the knowledge of Jesus with other people. I understood from Peter's great word (1 Peter 3:15) that it was possible to be 'ready to give an answer' when in natural circumstances friends, neighbours and workmates raised questions about my faith and lifestyle. In other words, I discovered the thrill of personal witnessing and the fascination of 'apologetics'; the reasoned defence of the Faith.

It seemed to me that most people cannot clearly see the Christian path because of the undergrowth that trails and creeps across it; the misconceptions and muddles which lead them to think the gospel unbelievable. Clearing the path by giving good reasons to believe, will not automatically guarantee that they *take* the path. But at least it presents them with a clear choice, not a confused one.

By now, I was a busy young preacher, too. This came

as a great surprise. A harassed church secretary dropped on me at short notice to 'give a testimony' because the booked preacher failed to turn up. I found an unsuspected facility with public speech, and within a month was taking engagements to give full half-hour sermons. The discovery was awesome. Elementary and barely-exercised as the gift was in my late teens, I found people visibly moved, helped, uplifted, even sometimes converted.

There were some uplifted eyebrows too. C S Lewis and Archbishop Trench were not often quoted in Gospel Halls in those days! The Sermon on the Mount was normally dismissed as 'Kingdom teaching' for a different era. But I'd been thrilled by Alexander Maclaren's handling of it. He tapped each verse with his golden hammer and it split into glowing segments of gospel truth. I tried it myself, in a series of Saturday youth nights, and people of my father's age asked if they could slip in at the back to listen.

Rita and I married at twenty-two, and our rented house became an unofficial HQ for a plethora of activities inside and outside the church. During daytime each of us had our employment. Evenings were spent deploying a whole team of our contemporaries or those a little younger. We ran church departments, helped at youth clubs, taught children's meetings, preached at adult services, and opened our home to a stream of fellow-workers and converts. But where was it all leading?

How God guides
Together we worked out a homespun philosophy of God's guidance in personal life. Starting-place was that

great challenge and promise from the Book of Proverbs: 'Trust in the LORD with all your heart and lean not on your own understanding. In all your ways acknowledge him and he will make your paths straight' (Proverbs 3:5-6). (The Authorised Version had 'he will direct your paths'.)

We understood this to mean that the sense of God's direction *in particular* comes to those who settle in *general* terms God's 'right' to have his way and work out his purpose. We willingly 'acknowledge' him to be Lord of every department in life. We are his, because he made us and because he has redeemed us at great cost. So, when a particular issue arises, we can dare to believe that he will intervene and direct, as we have already submitted to his rights in us.

How does the direction show itself? We came to think of a process of converging lines on a piece of paper. One is *prayer*: the daily sharing of life with God. One is *scripture*: the amount of God's revealed will particularly expressed in the words of the Bible is remarkable. You don't find it by sticking a pin in its pages, but by opening your life daily to biblical instruction and example. Then the truth you read last month becomes the light of God today when you especially need it.

Another is the *Holy Spirit*. In those pre-renewal days we had scarcely heard of the gifts of the Spirit. But we certainly knew that the Third Person of the Trinity indwells every believer, and that the mark of a child of God is the prompting of the Spirit of God. Enabling and ability granted by him was obviously part of that guidance.

Advice from godly friends was another 'line' to follow. We trusted those who held authority in the church, and they gave both public instruction and personal counsel. We were fortunate: I now suspect that those 'elders' (and often their godly wives) were a long way above average.

Harder to define and describe, but very real nevertheless, was *an inner sense* of ease or unease. 'The peace of God' (sensed or absent) acts as a kind of reference point within the heart and mind. Paul suggests this in Philippians 4:7.

Then came the whole issue of *circumstance and coincidence*. Since God is Lord of all creation, all that happens must in some sense be either 'sent' or at least 'allowed'. If some 'happenstance' (as our American friends cheerfully call it) converges on a point where the other lines already converge, surely this could be seen as some kind of confirmation.

Such rough guidelines had already served us well and given us a sense of moving together in God's purpose. Then, within a year of marriage, came the really big one.

A call to service

Happy and fruitful work kept me so busy that earning a living became almost a distraction. Yet I had long believed that 'secular work' done not merely as a bread-winning duty but 'to the glory of God' was the route for the great majority of Christians. One June morning, newspaper headlines leapt at me on my walk to the foundry. The story was a strange one. In the heat of a summer afternoon, lightning had struck at Ascot racecourse, stunning scores of people and killing several. One death was that of Leonard Tingle, an evangelist of the Open Air Mission, that society which had played such a decisive part in my own conversion one snowy January. At his burial service, high on a hillside above Sheffield (as I learned later) the officiating minister had gestured over the smoke-laden valley and said, 'Down there they struggle and fight to make gold. But up there (pointing to the sky) Len is walking on it.'

The powerful thought came to me ... 'Go and fill Len Tingle's shoes.' Rita and I had long talks together as we weighed the consequences. An evangelist's salary was less than half of what I was currently earning—and promotion was in the pipeline which would have claimed more of my time and left less for Christian work. We would have to move severely down-market in terms of residence.

We traced those 'lines of guidance' and found an increasing sense that they met at the office of the Open Air Mission (so to speak). Church elders were sure of my call to preaching and some were already wondering what next to do with me, as their church system offered very limited opportunity. (This, incidentally, is a constantly repeated story which has led to a huge haemorrhage over the generations from that movement to virtually every other Christian denomination. The number of ex-Brethren now prominent leaders in the Church of England, the Baptists and the Restoration churches is simply amazing.) Friends of our own age concurred, and gave wide-eyed promises of prayer support. A long interview with the Mission Committee satisfied them and us that there was no theological barrier. Two of their evangelists who knew me urged the committee to take me on board.

Rita, who would bear the brunt of frequent separation and comparative poverty, reminded me of the day we had stood at the Keswick Convention to surrender our lives to God's direction wherever it might lead. 'If the Lord calls us, he'll provide; we know that,' she said wistfully, as she looked around the living-room that would have to go, and squeezed my hand. 'Before we married, we agreed ... Anywhere with God.'

We took a further two months to pray, and ponder, then accepted the Mission's invitation. The sequel provided a startling confirmation. I gave 'two month's notice' at the foundry, and planned to begin my evangelistic career in January 1956. Two weeks later, hurrying around the shop-floor with my clipboard I collapsed with severe chest pains and was carried on an old door by four men back to my office. 'Spontaneous pneumathorax' said the doctor briskly. 'I've never seen it before until last week. I think I've done well to recognize it. Your left lung has collapsed. All those years of bronchial asthma have weakened it, and since the asthma disappeared you've gone mad with all your voluntary work. I'm afraid that one or the other will have to go: either give up your church work, or look for another job. What's that? You've already given your notice? There's a happy coincidence.' (How remarkable is God's timing—and sometimes how drastic are his confirmations!)

With God under an open sky
The next seven years were one continual adventure. The Open Air Mission sends its evangelists where the people are to be found, to tell them of God's saving love. Public executions were once popular venues for the crowds, and there the men with a message first found their audience. In the 1950's the venues were the great race-

courses of the land, the beaches in summer, the factory gates at lunch-time, the great fairs of Newcastle, Hull and Oxford. So were several historic debating places; Tower Hill and Hyde Park Corner in London, and their equivalents in Liverpool, Manchester and Birmingham. For seven years these were my pitches. Led by senior men of already wide experience, we 'junior men' had to learn the hard way, and learn quickly.

With senior colleague Willie Docherty, I travelled to the mill-towns of Yorkshire, the sooty streets of Lancashire, the high fells of Cumberland, the bleak coast of Aberdeenshire, and 'Barrowland' in Glasgow. The winter found us conducting small missions in churches and chapels. Under Willie Docherty's expert tuition I learned how to spin out a humorous story until the crowd thickened, how to think on my feet when the heckling grew hot, how to tell a children's story that pierced the defences of watching parents, and above all how to communicate the piercing biblical truth with effectiveness and power.

Two years later I became junior to Graham Stokes in marginally more cerebral enterprises. We took on the Secular Society in pitched verbal battles and debated evidences for the Resurrection, the reasonableness of faith, and apologetics in general. We gained access to school assemblies, and used slide travelogues in newly built community centres.

Then, surprisingly soon because of staff changes, the OAM made me a 'senior evangelist' and gave me my own caravan plus a younger colleague. My own beloved north-east of England became my main stamping-ground.

If it is permissible to use the word 'romance' in

describing the art of preaching, then the open-air variety must stand high in the romantic category. Here the whole kaleidoscope of human life passes by. Here are the coincidences of timing, subject and listeners circumstance, that can only be the footprints of the Holy Spirit. Here the Bible stands unique as the divine handbook of powerful and persuasive truth, applicable to an astounding variety of human needs and situations. I don't think that a week ever passed without some saving and transforming encounter with a human being who found God.

And then indoors

Itinerant evangelism was not my life-work. The main problem for me was the frustration of pointing passing people towards their first thoughts of God, but then leaving them to other people for nurture. I wanted to spend more time with them. I wanted to sit beside them with a Bible and show them its immeasurable riches. After seven years, that opportunity presented itself.

We held a two-week mission in Newcastle on Tyne. It was not outstandingly successful. Rough youths barracked the indoor services and had to be made to leave their cudgels and knives at the door. In this policing exercise we were considerably assisted by a fairground strongman who had turned to Christ as a result of having his pitch next to ours. But several teenagers were converted, and I lived near enough to follow them up with simple Bible-studies.

The church, then known as Eldon Evangelical (now Blaicklaw) had never employed a paid pastor in its seventy years, but was now considering that step. They asked me if I might be interested. I recalled a recent engagement in an Argyll parish church as pulpit-supply during a beach mission. The driver who took me there and back (a local businessman) kept glancing at my face afterwards and saying, 'You should be a Minister' (when a devout Scotsman says that, you can hear the capital 'M'). Baptists in my hometown kept saying it too. The thought began to captivate me.

We had a little boy by now, and another on the way. Leaving home for three weeks out of every four got no easier with practice. I was already following a London Bible College correspondence course for the Certificate of Proficiency in Religious Knowledge (in those days a requirement for teaching religion in schools, but also a part-qualification for the pastoral ministry of several denominations). Were the lines on the page beginning to converge on a crisis-point once more?

The Baptist ministry held a great appeal for me. Baptist understanding of leadership comes nowhere near that priestly-clerical-professionalism which Brethren so rightly fear (and yet tend wrongly to imagine to be fundamental to any style of leadership other than their own). When a kindly Area Superintendent interviewed me, his first question was, 'What makes you lean toward the pastoral ministry?' Without a pause to think, I replied, 'Its absence in the churches I move amongst.' He said it was the most interesting answer he'd heard for a long time. Only when I came out with the words did I realise that this was the heart of my restlessness.

I accepted the call to Eldon Evangelical Church as a salaried lay-pastor, on the understanding that I would be studying at the same time for qualification as a Baptist minister.

DONALD BRIDGE

God's grace among the Geordies

The Newcastle experience was thrilling, colourful, immensely rewarding and encouragingly fruitful. At my persuasion, we dropped the traditional concept of Sunday-evening 'gospel services' at which mission-type variations of the three R's were wont to be given (I mean, of course, Ruin, Redemption and Regeneration). Instead, I preached brief series on Bible doctrines, or longer series from Bible books. We looked at the doctrine of God, the Sermon on the Mount, the book of Jonah, the Acts of the Apostles, the meaning of New Birth, the way to Assurance, what it means to be a child of God, and the Epistle to the Romans.

The early *Banner of Truth* magazines and Puritan reprints were just appearing, and did much to fortify my conviction that the church's task is not just to 'preach the gospel' (within a strictly-defined decisionist framework) but rather *to declare the whole Word of God* and to apply it to everyday faith and behaviour.

It worked! Congregations grew from 40 to about 110, comfortably filling the modest building. We dug out our own baptistry at the front of the church, and several who excavated it were the first to be baptized within it. Conversions were regular. I recall one sermon, based on Christ's words, 'What shall it profit a man if he gain the whole world and lose his own soul?' That brought six different people to me that week for counsel, prayer and new birth. The sequel was amusing. My homiletics course with the Baptist Union was lagging slightly. For homework that week, I was required to submit a written sermon on 'the value of the soul'. I cheated, and simply sent in a scribbled version of this talk. The tutor gave me rather poor marks, and complained that it 'lacked contemporary relevance'. I wondered mischievously what could be more contemporarily relevant than six conversions!

Parallel to the preaching was an immense amount of pastoral visitation and personal counselling. I never became a kind of religious social-worker (the cul-de-sac that I fear some clergy have drifted into). But I found that the preaching and teaching stirred people to ask questions which they had never faced up to before. How can this work in my life? Why is my experience of prayer so shallow? What are the implications of saying that God made me? Why am I not a better husband? Why does God allow suffering? What am I to make of this new 'permissiveness'?

We were now in the swinging sixties, that appalling slide into subjectivism, secularism and abandonment of absolutes, that would have such devastating consequences on every area of Britain's life for the next thirty years. Christians needed to see all of this in a biblical light, and non-Christians needed to be warned of its inevitable harvest. That meant hours of personal discipling as well as half-hours of earnest preaching.

The four years in Newcastle were good and happy. I ended them with deeper convictions than ever about the eternal relevance of the Bible. And my vocation to teach, explain, declare and apply it to human life seemed clearer than ever.

From Tyne to Wear
Sunderland is only eleven miles south-east of Newcastle, but the change is drastic. Never describe a Sunderland

man as a Geordie: it is historically inaccurate and racially abusive! The newly-built Baptist church (replacing a gaunt chapel demolished by area demolition and rebuilding) stood on the north bank of the Wear, its slim wooden cross dwarfed by the towering shipyard cranes. Here in a simple, solemn ceremony which marked a deepening of my sense of vocation, I was ordained into the Baptist ministry.

It was another expression of the converging lines. For Baptists, ordination is a public recognition of several threads that run through the life and leadership of the local and worldwide church. I related my experience of conversion, guidance and calling. The Sunderland church leaders described how they had been led to invite me to the pastorate. Evidence was given of my progress in studies and my modest achievements therein (the subjects were New Testament Greek, Church History, Bible Knowledge, and my own chosen topic of the Person and Work of Christ). Testimony was shared of God's touch in people's lives through my preaching. Representatives of the wider church joined with local leaders in sharing with me the laying-on of hands. Its meaning?—An expression of corporate fellowship and a prayer for divine anointing.

The next seven years realized every hope that such an anointing was offered and received. All my hammered-out convictions were tested and confirmed: convictions about the unique authority of the Bible, the power of a life-changing gospel, the importance of a loving, structured fellowship.

There were new convictions too. Or perhaps it was new clarity in already half-formed convictions: the need to restore worship at the heart of church life; the vibrant reality of Holy Spirit renewal; the place of a sensitive, healing ministry (preferably alongside qualified doctors).

Explore the Word

Above all my conviction that I was called to explain, expound and apply the Word of God reached its fuller expression. The Bible is a great united collection of divinely inspired books, not a treasure-chest of isolated favourite texts. To unpack those books in simple, systematic and forceful explanation is a never-ending exercise in learning together from God. Being systematic, it rescues the preacher and protects the hearers from the treadmill of the minister's favourite texts and topics. It also protects the preacher from the wrath of his hearers when they hear messages which they feel to be too personal, painful or pertinent. The expositor has a perfect alibi. 'We reached the end of chapter 3 last week; now we come to chapter 4, and this is what it says.'

Again and again the growing congregation welcomed and embraced (often with astonishment) the words that proved to be indeed words from God. One does not have to keep arguing for the doctrine of biblical inspiration. It has its own divinely-working effect. In Sunderland I proved that repeatedly. The pews were filled, extra seats were needed in the aisles most Sundays, and the water of the lovely open baptistry beneath the cross was constantly disturbed by those who were drawn to faith and obedience.

Moving Southwards

The realization that a local ministry is ending resembles the sudden dropping of a shutter. In autumn 1971 I took up the post-holiday church programme—and found that there was no shining path ahead. The voice divine was calling us on—to our surprise and the church's.

Baptists have their own way of moving ministers. It involves a superintendent's list, quiet winks and nods, private interviews, discreet moves by spies and talent-spotters, and eventually several invitations to preach. In a remarkably short time I received a call from Frinton Free Church in Essex. *I* had a wistful vision of what the influence of a strong church in a small community might accomplish. *They* were seeking someone with biblical and evangelistic experience who might lead them into new church-planting as the town expanded. Once more the lines were converging. The farewell to Enon Church was emotional and painful. Love can be quite wearing!

Two dissimilar places; a northern city and an Essex small town with a reputation for elitism. When our family arrived we found ourselves whispering because the tree-lined avenues were so quiet. The church manse had once been a holiday-retreat for the actress Gladys Cooper, and Noel Coward was often seen there (presumably asking 'anyone for tennis?' since the tennis club and the cricket club dominated the social life).

In fact the town was expanding, with many young commuters willing to travel ninety minutes into London for work. Only a few children and teenagers attended, and the congregation was mainly elderly. But it was what would later be called a classic church-growth situation. The church was destined to be thronged with people of all ages.

I had no clear programme. I simply carried on my conviction that the scriptures declared and applied within an affectionate, worshipping fellowship, would draw people to faith and service. Exactly that happened. The next twelve years provided a breathless saga of growth, commitment, expansion and adventure. Many years later I was told that north-east Essex is beginning to be called the New Bible Belt of Britain, and that much of this was attributed to what happened amongst Baptists and Anglicans during those breathless days (not all, or course, through my personal ministry). But in our church we saw hundreds profess conversion.

Many of these converts joined our membership (I recall the five-hundredth being recognized in my tenth year). Others joined the new church which we planted in due course and, as hoped, it flourished. Others threw in their lot with churches nearer their homes, in surrounding villages or nearby towns like Walton and Clacton. I discovered that two churches in other counties were using tapes of Frinton sermons the following week in their evening services, instead of a live preacher, and that some remarkable growth had followed. To cap that whole slightly bizarre story, several hundred tapes were used in the Anglican cathedral of a South American capital.

The pain of change

This meant constant change, and not all of it was welcome. I have never deliberately instigated change; rather I have found that what God was doing pressed constant adjustment on me and on my people. It can be very threatening. It robs us of comfortable predictables. It poses searching questions about cherished traditions and practices that have long-since ceased to be relevant or even helpful. Most painful for me personally was the fact that my role within the leadership had to be redefined and readjusted several times. Those who had invited me to be their minister discovered that my role changed before their eyes—some did not like it. I myself had to accept changing methods of nurture and teaching that moved in the direction of small groups (not really my scene).

But painful and wearing though some of this was, it marked life and vitality. You cannot grow and remain unchanged at the same time!

Frinton added a fresh conviction to my ministry. New converts make the most effective witnesses. Give them a predictable standard of worship, preaching and fellowship—and *they* will bring in the people. 1972-1984 were great years. And then the lines began to part—to converge later in a startling new pattern.

Rita and I had a growing sense of being 'burned out'. I was able to pay very few visits to other churches because of the demands of my own. I was now writing occasional books of popular theology (restricting this to one three-hour period per week). Returning from a rare engagement at a one-week Bible convention I discovered that sudden lack of direction and energy once more.

The lure of the Holy Land
Rita and I knew Israel and loved it. We had already conducted pilgrimage tours there, and the church had sent me on a summer sabbatical to study biblical archaeology. We were truly smitten by that lovely land where one can so literally walk in the footsteps of Jesus.

Bishop George Goodwin-Hudson, who slipped into

our congregation occasionally, had a long talk with me. The Garden Tomb Association based in Jerusalem was at a turning-point in a number of ways. They needed a chaplain and on-the-spot director for a longer period than the usual three-to-six months. Regular Bible preaching to a large, constantly changing congregation was needed, as well as high-level contacts with the colourful and variegated religious traditions in the city. But there would also be ample time for studying and writing.

Now I need to interrupt myself and say something about writing. Back in the early days of 'Renewal' in the Sunderland of the 1970's, I had preached a series of sermons on the Holy Spirit, his person and work, his fruit and his gifts. David Phypers, a deacon, urged me to put them into print. I tried one or two and soon discovered that writing and speaking are quite different arts, requiring different shapes and skills. I wanted to drop the idea, but David suggested that we do a joint venture. By the time we had found a publisher (after several rejections) I had moved on to Frinton and David had become an Anglican vicar in Derby.

Spiritual Gifts and the Church, published by IVP in 1973 and brave they were to do it, caught a tide of opinion and need. It was a good-seller, but not a bestseller. It went into several UK editions, two in America, and one in Indonesia. To our surprise several thousand Christians and several hundred churches professed significant change in understanding or direction through its influence.

When a publisher accepts a new writer, a contract is offered which sometimes gives that publisher first choice of the next manuscript. Next? We saw possibilities. Two writers of evangelical conviction but different denominational loyalty could write eirenic works on potentially-divisive topics, always revolving around the ultimate authority of scripture.

Book followed book, on Baptism, Communion, Charismatic Renewal and Christian Discipling. The method was to write alternate chapters—and then re-write each other's. After five books we ended the partnership (amicably, I hasten to say) and wrote separately. I continued with a biography of Ernest Luff (a Frinton hero) and a book on 'Signs and Wonders'. Publishers were pressing me to look at the neglected subject of Church Discipline, and I had thoughts about Power Evangelism. Scripture Union engaged me to write some of their daily Bible-notes for a large readership; something I loved. And that brings me round to Israel again. There I would have more time to write. There I could lay the basis for a kind of trouble-shooting consultant ministry (Have Bible, Will Travel).

Living in the Promised Land

The fourteen months in Israel were unique and unforgettable. I've described them elsewhere, more than once. In an almost uncanny way, we discovered that we had 'come home'. Jerusalem does not impact every Christian that way, and unfortunately some whom it does are embarrassing enthusiasts, if not outright cranks. The evangelical leaders in the city shared a rueful saying: if a stranger assures you that God has told him to come to Jerusalem, run for cover!

To preach in the Land of the Book was a moving experience. To someone whose mind had been immersed in scripture from youth and whose imagination had been coloured by biblical scenes for a lifetime, residence in Israel offered constant fascination. The overwhelming impression is of vital connection between Land and Book. Both of them are like semi-incarnations of the invisible God, preparing the way for his coming who was indeed the Word made flesh.

Men sit patiently by the road, waiting to be hired as day labourers. A Jewish family hurry to worship at the temple wall, father instructing his children in the truth as they skip along. Galilee fishermen deploy both cast-nets and drag-nets exactly as did the sons of Zebedee. The tombs of the prophets shine in the sun, visible from the rabbi-staircase where Jesus denounced some of the religious leaders. A line of mikvaot (ritual immersion pools) are found near the temple ruins; enough to baptize three thousand. An almond tree blossoms early in our garden, with its punning promise that God will watch over his Word to fulfil it. Still water lies in the pool of Bethesda but Siloam is a moving pool with entry and exit. Sheep and goats together kick up such a cloud of dust that they are indistinguishable (and the shepherd walks ahead, not behind). Do you recognize these Bible-references, as I did (and hundreds more) with almost heart-stopping emotion?

On our welcome 'days off' (one each week, and three together every six weeks) we explored further afield, with Bible in one hand and map in the other. We traced the steps of Abraham, Samson, David, Isaiah, Peter and Philip. Most of all we walked in the steps of Jesus, and were overwhelmed with the realization repeatedly refreshed, that he was truly human, truly Jewish, truly a

Galilean ... and yet the eternal Son, yesterday, today and forever the same.

To centre my preaching in Jesus' Jerusalem was truly awesome. My outdoor congregations were composed of tourists, with a few local Christians plus our dozen staff. They came from every country and continent, and numbered anything from fifty to five hundred—sometimes very many more.

The Garden Tomb is a superb place to expound Old and New Testament together, in their inseparable connections. Jewish and Christian feasts and festivals also offered colourful topics. Easter and Passover coincided that year, so Whit and Pentecost coincided too. Yom Kippur (the solemn Day of Atonement) offered splendid opportunity to explain the high priesthood of Jesus. Christmas and Hanukkah pointed us to the coming of the Light of the World.

The Garden Tomb is never presented as the only possible site for the great Easter events, but rather as a superb visual aid to the gospel story. Many people had their faith renewed or confirmed. Many spoke of having found Christ for the first time. The famous and the infamous from international politics, entertainment, education and religion, discussed Truth with me. This led to more invitations to travel worldwide with the message than I could always accept. Meanwhile there was time to write on Power Evangelism, on Church Discipline and on the problem of Doubt.

Europe and America
By the end of 1985 my term of service ended. Home once more in England, we were able to continue that ministry

of consultancy, trouble-shooting and leadership training that has kept me occupied ever since. It has taken me
to new churches in Belgium, to startlingly big churches
in many American states, to Brethren churches in Scotland moving into thrilling growth. Now, resident in
Durham's lovely city, Rita and I work with the Northern
Baptist Association, with Brethren Partnership, and under the banner of The Evangelization Society. Our great
concern remains the same: to assist in mission, to consult
in leadership, to steer through the pitfalls of 'change'
and to promote evangelical, expository Bible preaching
by example, training and writing.

It has been a convoluted path that we have pursued
together since those days in Stockton when we learned
together to follow the divine beckoning hand. Some
changes of direction have puzzled our friends. Some
have puzzled us too! But we believe that in God's sight
the whole journey has been a straight line.

Am I supposed to be an evangelist, a minister, an
author, a chaplain, or a consultant? All I can say is,
'God's Word grips me and drives me on, virtually preaching itself through me. I want to be faithful to its motives,
its message, and its vision of Christ.'

Some words read in my teens (the author forgotten if
I ever knew) have come back to me again and again.

> Christ the Son of God has sent me
> to the midnight lands;
> Mine the mighty ordination
> of the pierced hands.

2

HEROES, MENTORS AND FRIENDS

Lorimer Gray

Heroes become mentors when their personal influence creates positive changes in your attitudes and behaviour. Friends can do that too. All three have had an important part to play in the life of Lorimer Gray.

When I was young, I had many heroes. Rupert Bear, the Lone Ranger and many other cowboys like him inspired me and coloured my thinking and playing, if only for a fleeting moment, in those growing years. I worked hard at having the 'fastest draw' amongst my childhood cowboy friends, I searched for adventure with the Famous Five, I longed to play rugby for Scotland like Sandy Carmichael or 'Beastie' MacLaughlan. Clint Eastwood is still a hero today.

But more important than the influence of heroes has been the impact of mentors. Men and women whose personalities and influence God used to bring about change and introduce quality to the life of a young man not obviously endowed with an academic bent, as others in my family. But I had a vibrant enthusiasm for life, particularly to share with those fellow human-beings who made up my ever-widening circle of friends. And what an important part those mentors have had in helping hone my direction and eventual calling to full-time Christian service! Along the way their influence has challenged and stimulated, corrected and encouraged, coached and educated me so that I never felt the lack of a formal college training. I was compensated by the informal educational experience of the 'university of real life'.

Friends, too, played a very important part in preparing the ground for my future. Many heroes and mentors became close friends, and some of my friends, gathered along the way, became mentors and heroes. Clearly those marvellous people have had a profound effect in helping to develop in me qualities of Christian leadership which have been of great benefit to me and, I hope, to others.

A Christian family

Life in the Gray household was a very happy experience. My parents, Andrew and Lois, had lived in the family home on the south side of Glasgow since their marriage during the Second World War. Along with my elder sister, Elspeth, and younger brother, Nicholas, we enjoyed a very organised, almost regimented, middle-class family routine. Breakfast was at 7.45 am, evening meal at 6 pm and Sunday lunch was, of course, always a 'Sunday joint' with a good pudding to follow. The laws of the Medes and the Persians ruled with regard to time and it is now sometimes hard to believe that the strictly disciplined routines of those days resulted in such a 'secure' environment. Strangely enough it seemed to work.

The Christian way of life was an integral part of our family life and on Sundays 'homeless students' would join us for lunch after church. Home life for the Grays was normally a colourful mixture of sport and study, music and laughter, visitors and friendships, loving acceptance and mutual encouragement.

My parents were very much involved in their local church and many other evangelical Christian activities in the Glasgow area. As a prominent and gifted preacher within the independent evangelical church movement known as the Christian Brethren, my father was much in demand as a speaker for services as well as committee work. Both he and my mother were also deeply involved in overseas missionary work, often welcoming missionaries, home on leave, to stay in the family home. With that kind of background, it was almost inevitable that all three children should, at some stage, commit their own lives to the service of Jesus Christ. And of course, for me, that was the beginning of a spiritual adventure which started at a Crusader camp in Aviemore in the Scottish Highlands and is continuing in a Christian outdoor centre in Nethybridge, some 10 miles further up the Spey Valley.

Teenage years
I attended the High School of Glasgow—an institution which dates back to the 12th century and offered a good all-round education for boys from a wide spectrum of social backgrounds. For me, they were good days, although after 13 years at the one establishment, I suffered a distinct shortage of paper qualifications. On one occasion, my distraught mother was invited to meet my class teacher. 'Mrs Gray,' she said, 'Your son will manage to overcome most educational hurdles by his sheer enthusiasm for living!' Little did she know how prophetic that statement would need to be!

Extra-curricular activities at the High School were in abundance and these had much greater appeal to a schoolboy like Master Gray. Study seemed an unnecessary adjunct to the excitement of living and in the earlier years of the secondary department provided a monotonous fill-in between rugby training and various clubs and societies. In my final year, signs of management skills were becoming evident, for although the Headmaster thought *he* managed the school, the Council of Prefects under the leadership of my close friend, Chris Thomson, and myself, actually directed the entire school operation. Or so we liked to believe!

During these teenage years, leadership fell naturally on to my shoulders. Numerous Christian activities filled my evenings and weekends. Scripture Union rallies were a monthly highlight throughout the winter, led for years by my friends and me. For a long time, Cliff Barrows, of the Billy Graham Evangelistic Team, had been another of my heroes, mainly through his ability to conduct large gatherings of people in singing Christian songs. For hours, in front of the full-length mirror in my parents' bedroom, I would practise 3 and 4-beat Christian songs, with arms waving to emulate the style of my hero. It was essential to have 'white cuffs' and ensure your arms moved from shoulder height upwards. The SU rallies were where I put this into practice. What a thrill to lead hundreds in praising God! But because it was normally very warm and very physical—it was never possible to remove your jacket—the sweat of hard effort was all too obvious!

Crusaders—the then 'all boys' Bible class movement—gave me a first-class opportunity to develop Bible teaching skills, using the 'do-it and learn-from-your-mistakes' method. I remember, at the age of 17, having to give a talk on a series from T C Hammond's book, *In Understanding Be Men*. My given topic was 'Kenosis and the Hypostatic Union of the Lord Jesus'. A fascinating subject both for me and the other 16-year old lads in the group! Help!

Various committees and youth activities broadened my understanding of Christian work whilst youth out-reach cafes, speaking engagements and a busy church-life involvement gave me a wealth of resources for future ministry.

Two Christian mentors played vital parts at this stage— Oswald Carvel and Norman Walker. Little did I know then that, one day in the future, both of these men who influenced my teenage years would be used by God to introduce me to the specific calling of the Abernethy Outdoor Centres in Scotland. As leaders, they demon-strated tremendous charisma, reflecting a vital zeal for winning boys for Jesus Christ.

Oswald was a great role model and I attempted to reproduce his enthusiasm for singing by copying his style. He always sang very loudly in the Crusader class, creating an impression that singing was acceptable and manly, particularly relevant to a boys' group under peer pressure not to participate. And it did the trick, and I have copied it for years. He always talked about boys as 'men' making us feel grown-up and important. His quality of spiritual life combined with his strong interest in outdoor pursuits, particularly the mountains, fired me up as a young man and sowed the seeds of what has eventually become part of my calling. Little did I know then that one day he would be my boss.

In 1960 at that Aviemore Crusader Camp when I genuinely handed over the running of my life to the Lord Jesus , Norman Walker was a role model for all of us. Strong, fit and competitive, he set the pace in mountain trekking and sailing. In those days, qualifications and equipment were not as vital as they are today, but adventure and challenge were high on the agenda. Norman provided both and used them effectively to illustrate the importance and vitality of being a Christian.

A few years later, in 1964, another specialist activity holiday was organised by Crusaders at the Scottish Sports Council Centre at the foot of the Cairngorms. Norman was again one of the leaders of the holiday, appropriately entitled 'Go Glenmore in '64'. God spoke to him very clearly during that fortnight, giving him a vision to set up a similar outdoor centre but with a definite evangelistic Christian purpose. It took a further seven years before that dream became a reality as the Abernethy Outdoor Centre.

Norman falls into that category of Christian leaders who often, without knowing it, motivate and inspire simply by their presence and conversation. Throughout the years of knowing him, I have seldom come away from being in his presence without feeling encouraged or re-motivated to strive for higher achievements. A very special gift.

I know there are many in Christian work today who have been strongly influenced for God by these men. I am proud to be part of that group and even now am continually inspired by them both as they mentor me in my role at Abernethy.

Throughout these special teenage years, a whole

multitude of other short-term heroes and mentors played their part in my moulding process. I was fortunate to be given responsibility early on—with hindsight, maybe too much—but I relished the opportunities and blossomed as a result, although with each new Christian commitment, academic school work became even less interesting. However, some higher education results were achieved but nowhere near enough to take me on to university. Maybe that was all part of God's plan, or possibly I have rationalised my own lack of application!

My parents were clearly disappointed and I think a little confused. The other two Gray children were clearly destined for good degrees but middle son, Lorimer, although doing well in Christian things, was proving a bit of a slow starter, to put it mildly, in educational matters. My problem was that study seemed so irrelevant to the main business of living and particularly in comparison to my enthusiasm for Christian work. On reflection, my parents, like most parents, wanted me to be an achiever and, within the confines of our family experience, that meant getting a university degree. Thankfully they didn't give up on me and we began to explore other possibilities.

Finding a job
The options were limited—accountancy, surveying, banking or insurance. An apprenticeship in quantity surveying seemed the best bet. Day-release, evening classes, out on building sites, bricks and mortar, lots of fresh air and the princely sum of £9 a month salary! So in 1965 I applied for and subsequently accepted the job as a first-year apprentice.

Mentor number three was Mr W H Dinsmore, the senior partner of a well-established quantity surveying firm in the centre of Glasgow. Affectionately known by all of the apprentices as 'Big Will', he ruled the practice with a rod of iron, demanding quality work, accuracy in detail and complete loyalty to his firm. The life of an apprentice was tough but the mentoring of Mr Dinsmore was quite critical in developing in me qualities and strengths new to a recent school-leaver. My face seemed to fit and this was reflected in that within the boring list of first-year apprenticeship responsibilities, I was given the privilege of driving Big Will's Humber Supersnipe from one parking meter to another, at his request.

Three and a half years of apprenticeship later, I could have been qualified as a sanitary inspector if I had bothered to pay the appropriate Institute fees. But I had become exceedingly bored and extremely frustrated with figures, materials and constant paperwork. One Monday in March I noticed an interesting advertisement in the *Glasgow Herald* for a personnel assistant with a large American engineering company in Uddingston, called Caterpillar Tractors. Secretly I wrote away for more information and an application form. I remembered having visited the factory as a boy with my Bible class many years before. There was a real sense of excitement as I waited. Would they reply? Was my letter of interest? What would my parents think? Or for that matter, what would 'Big Will' say? A change of career ... into what? Personnel Management? I waited patiently for a reply to my letter.

A friend and life partner

Around this time, another very important influence began to play a significant part in my life. Moira MacPhail was her name. Girls had already featured in my small world for some years, providing an interesting contrast to the monastic existence of an all-boys school where the only distractions were the young school secretary and the temporary French language assistant.

I think I had fairly clear ideas about the sort of girlfriend I wanted. Being a practical sort of chap, I had naively drawn up a long list of requirements for the ideal mate, then with youthful, spiritual fervour, I had asked God to bless the list and bring along Miss Right. What a relief it was to know that God had a good sense of humour! Overlooking my theologically doubtful approach to guidance, he heard my prayer and answered it in his way and in his time. After a number of experiments with some very charming and patient members of the fairer sex, it inevitably became clear that Moira MacPhail far exceeded the hopes and expectations I might have had. So with nothing to lose, I set about the task of getting to know her.

Our friendship grew over a number of years and was greatly helped by the fact that both sets of parents knew each other very well and had been friends for years. Moira and I first met when we were just 2 or 3 years old at a joint family picnic on the beach at Troon in Ayrshire. Many picnics and many years later, on that same beach at Troon, I asked Moira to marry me. Her astonishing answer of 'Yes' made up for the unpleasant salty water stain on my neatly pressed trousers from kneeling in the sand!

Our common enthusiasm for sports and outdoor pursuits encouraged our relationship. There was skiing in the winter, with tennis and sailing in the summer, although it was the latter that almost capsized our relationship. When we started going out with one another, Moira was already qualified as a sailing instructor, but without a boat. I owned the sailing dinghy. As the owner, I naturally wanted to helm the boat. But Moira knew more about sailing than I knew about anything! The scene was set for World War III. Thankfully we sold the boat to pay our legal fees ... on a house purchase.

Moira was already a committed Christian before we started to go out with each other. There was no doubt that we wanted to serve God as individuals and as a couple in our home churches and in joint projects. In those days, there were many opportunities for doing that in such activities as the Scripture Union youth rallies, Crusader activities, youth clubs and numerous Bible study groups. Life seemed to be very hectic, yet within all the busyness of careers, sports and Christian service, God was developing gifts and experience which he would use in the years ahead. How could we know that Moira's training in dietetics and institutional management, and my surveying skills, particularly building drawing, would all be used in our eventual involvement within the Abernethy Trust?

Personal growth and development
Moira understood my frustration with quantity surveying. We waited patiently to find out whether Caterpillar were interested. At last the envelope arrived and I was invited for interview. The whole selection process lasted

for a period of six weeks and it was during the second series of interviews that I met my mentor number four. Nelson Brown had been the Personnel Manager since the Caterpillar Tractor Company first opened its factory in 1959, and when I met him I immediately experienced a chemistry of affinity with him, a bond which has developed and matured into a deep, almost father-son relationship. He offered me the job and at the beginning of May 1969, the next phase of my 'university of real life' training began.

Nelson Brown's influence on me has been outstanding. Twenty years my senior, somehow he recognised within me the seeds of a potential 'people' manager. However, to achieve that end, much reconstruction work in me was necessary. Fundamentally, I was naive, blinkered in outlook, and very limited in my understanding and awareness of myself. Nelson has always said, 'If you ever want to analyse, understand and counsel other people, you need to understand yourself first.' His objective was clear. Using the day-to-day life of a busy personnel department serving 1,500 engineering employees, Nelson gently exposed my personality, and particularly my mind, to a whole range of fresh ideas and stimulating experiences, building on each, in the hope of creating a more open, balanced and better-equipped individual.

Nelson didn't let me off with the easy trite answers I had been used to giving as a narrow-minded, yet often apparently confident, evangelical. He probed and tirelessly drew out views and opinions, yet all the time encouraging personal growth and development. Over that period, he never once criticised my faith, but forced me to re-affirm it, based on solid argument and Biblical principle.

I am greatly indebted to a man who unselfishly committed himself to role modelling and faithful coaching over those intensive early years in the '70's. He continues to influence my thinking today. Not only is he my mentor but, thankfully, he is also still my close friend.

At long last the white envelope with 'Caterpillar' boldly printed in yellow and black popped through the letter box. Inside, the important words read 'We would like you to join us on May 16th at 8.30 am.' It was with a strange mixture of excitement and nervous tension that I borrowed my mother's car and drove to Uddingston, not realising that this was the first definite step towards a change of career and another springboard towards full-time Christian service.

My three years at Caterpillar were rich in valuable experiences and almost impossible to measure in terms of my personal development and the building of my character. On my first day, I was faced with a major problem: 'You know that this is an American company,' they said proudly. 'Americans don't like long names and "Lorimer" is not only long but a bit strange—so we'll just call you "Lori" from now on.' I still think that they chose the new abbreviated name because the Company made earth-moving equipment!

I learnt so much about people—all sorts of shapes, sizes, backgrounds, religions, genders and persuasions. Industrial relations and training were high on the agenda at Caterpillar and I was surrounded by professionals who willingly shared of themselves and their experiences. I seemed to be in the right place at the right time in this new working environment. As promotion opportunities arose for new challenges within the personnel department as people left, I was given the chance to progress. With alacrity and enthusiasm (and a lot of help from my mentor, Nelson Brown) I gave those challenges my best shot.

God was very faithful and honoured my desire to represent him in each situation as it arose, as well as helping me strive to do a good job. Many opportunities arose for me to share my faith and as I developed into a more complete person, God seemed to be underlining my growing usefulness for him. But it wasn't long before times at Caterpillar became hard with recession and redundancy. God had changes ahead for me.

Sense of calling

As an apprentice quantity surveyor and trainee personnel manager, I made my summer holidays a highlight of the year. Unlike my university friends who appeared to have half the year as their holidays, my three weeks seemed very precious. Once we were married, Moira and I usually spent at least two weeks of it on the west coast of Scotland. On one particular year, we joined up with some good friends of ours, Tony and Rosas Mitchell and their young family, in the little village of Arisaig. Two important things happened that summer.

One evening as the four of us sat in our caravan enjoying the sunset, our conversation moved round to the topic of what were we going to do in the years ahead. Each of us began to unpack our dreams. As the conversation developed, it became clear that the seeds of being involved in some kind of Christian outdoor centre ministry was on our hearts. Little did Tony and Rosas know then that before very long Moira and I would be seriously considering getting involved in a new venture that had been started in Nethybridge by Norman Walker, my boyhood mentor.

On the Sunday of that holiday, we attended the local Church of Scotland service. A creche facility was provided for parents with younger children. As I made my way out to the church hall, I came face to face with another young father, also on holiday in the area and heading towards the creche. It was Ian Leitch, the well-known Scottish evangelist. We established an immediate rapport and a friendship began that has grown and developed over the last 20 years. Ian's influence on the work of the Abernethy Centres in Scotland has been very important. His ministry has affected many of our lives and we often quote his illustrations to emphasise Biblical truth and practical application. Jimmy Thomson, Abernethy's long serving maintenance engineer, dates the beginning of his spiritual walk with God to Ian's visits to Abernethy in the early '80's. Just two more examples of friends who became mentors, facilitating critical stages in God's plans for me and the future of the Abernethy work.

During our early married years, Moira and I continued with our commitments amongst young people both in our church and local Crusader groups. In those early '70's, opportunities for Christian service were in abundance through evangelistic events involving people like Arthur Blessitt, Billy Graham and gospel outreach concerts. The counselling training and injection of enthusiasm for outreach were so vital to us both in those days and in preparing the ground for later years. So often, with hindsight, we look back and see clearly God at work preparing us for future assignments. If only we had been more aware at the time!

Move to England

To a Glaswegian, the idea of working in Edinburgh was almost alien to me. However, when in 1972 the Scotsman Publications, part of Thomson Regional Newspapers, invited me to join their personnel department in offices just off the Royal Mile, it seemed just the right thing to do. Training, and particularly supervisory management education, were important ingredients of the job description. By now, I was in the process of qualifying as a Member of the Institute of Personnel Management, with two of my chosen subjects being education and training. The new job was right up my street. As a family we moved lock, stock and barrel from East Kilbride to the south side of Edinburgh—but only for a short fourteen months. Another move was in the Master's plan.

Thomson Regional Newspapers required a personnel manager in Reading. 'Would I consider a transfer and promotion to the south of England?' they asked. Double the salary, company car, all expenses paid—but Reading! What a dilemma! Ambition versus family. New challenge in the south of England against developing Christian work in Edinburgh. Financial gain and personal stimulation contrasted with good church life and a developing circle of friends. Moira was very supportive and acknowledged with a look of relief in her eyes—it might have been somewhere much worse!

The new job was a real challenge. My boss was called Howard Green—a practising Roman Catholic for whom religious activity was very important. My role as personnel manager within this 400-employee newspaper company was to manage, in every sense, the development of the human resources employed by Thames Valley Newspapers Ltd. The challenge was enhanced by Howard Green's view that the personnel manager was also his executive assistant. In this role I became involved in a wide variety of other jobs, some of which were experiences never to be missed.

One of the strangest occurred at Christmas time. 'I would like to buy a Christmas present for each of my senior managers ... and their wives as well,' announced Mr Green to me one morning in December. Ten managers, I murmured to myself, with a sinking feeling. 'For the wives I thought a bottle of perfume might be a good idea,' and as an afterthought, 'Try and match the perfumes to the wives involved!' Some hours later, standing at the French perfume counter of the local upmarket department store, surrounded by sales assistants, I explained my dilemma. Ten lovely ladies—ten different perfumes—ten estimated ages. Help!

The whole Reading experience was invaluable. From a business standpoint I had to learn about the management of a department, budgetary control, management accounts, staff selection, disciplinary procedures, business plans and, of course, perfume selection. Our family was enjoying another lively church fellowship and all the trappings of an executive lifestyle—big house, two cars, a suit for every day of the week and 'food buying' in Marks and Spencer! But within our hearts, there was unrest and a sense of a 'calling' as yet unanswered. Within the Thomson Newspaper Group, the next move might have been to Cardiff, Newcastle or even Belfast. Just another rung or two up the corporate ladder. But it was already losing its gloss and shine. What did John 10:10 (GNB) really mean to us as a family?—'Life in all its fullness'. How could we combine our work efforts and our Christian service to glorify God and reach others with that message? Around the corner God had the answer to that longing in our hearts.

God opens the door
In 1971 the Abernethy Trust was formed. Norman Walker's vision to set up a Christian outdoor centre in Scotland had been on his heart since 1964. Surrounded by a group of Christian men and women who had caught hold of this same vision, he created a limited company with charitable status based on the House of Abernethy in Nethybridge. The property had once been the parish manse for the local church but had been sold into private hands some 40 years before. The building was in excellent condition and within the 30-acre estate, there already existed two staff cottages plus the old steading buildings where some of the original basic camps were held.

The work started slowly with many of the teething problems associated with such an innovative Christian outreach ministry. The inevitable conflict of providing a high quality programme of outdoor activities versus the economic viability of such a programme created enormous headaches. The board of directors and many others associated with this new exciting project, volunteered endless hours of their time and what must have seemed like vast sums of money to get the new work up and running. Different people were appointed for both short and longer term periods of time. Each played their part in helping to establish the work. There is no doubt those early years of hard graft created solid foundations for building the work in the years ahead.

As we travelled back from our family holiday, visiting Moira's parents in their home in Macduff, we took the opportunity of calling in at Nethybridge en route for Reading. Oswald Carvel, the then chairman of the directors, was holding the fort for the warden of the centre who was on holiday. It was a great pleasure to renew friendship with Oswald again after so many years, but we were saddened to hear that all was not well within the life of the Abernethy Outdoor Centre. Oswald explained to us that a series of difficulties had arisen, particularly of a relational nature between the staff, and that the centre hadn't really taken off quite in the direction that the directors had hoped it would by this stage. For one reason or another, progress had been slow. As a board, they were taking stock of the situation at that time.

As Moira and I walked around the grounds with Oswald, neither of us wished to voice it, but both of us had that sense of excitement beginning to build inside us. Towards the end of our visit, Oswald tentatively asked us whether we had considered the possibility of becoming involved in more of a full-time capacity with Abernethy. You could have knocked us over with a feather. For years we had been associated with Crusaders and Scripture Union, and had kept in touch with the developing Abernethy work. Could this be God opening a door through which he wanted us, not only to look but to take some major steps for him? We agreed with Oswald that we would return to Reading, praying and discussing, and planning to meet with him again in a few months' time.

Through a series of practical incidents culminating in my predecessor at Abernethy resigning from his post, Moira and I became very sure that God wanted us to explore more fully whether it was his will for us to be the next resident directors of the Abernethy Outdoor Centre.

We both attended an interview in Glasgow in March 1975. I have never had such an intensive grilling in my life. We were interviewed together, we were interviewed separately, our theological positions were checked and our table manners were carefully scrutinised during lunch, halfway through the four-hour interview. Not only was it a great relief to be asked by the directors to consider taking on the job of leading the work at Abernethy, but it was also reassuring to know that they had been unanimous in their decision to offer us the appointment. This would be very important, particularly in the early days of taking up the challenge of directing the work.

The folk in Reading were very supportive and some even envious of this move into meaningful outdoor centre work. Howard Green, my boss, encouraged me in every way possible—I hope to this day that it wasn't because I chose the wrong perfume for his wife the Christmas before! The bigger problem was explaining to my parents about our plans. Although they had been heavily involved in missionary work for many, many years, it was one thing for other people's children to be involved in such work, but initially it seemed quite a different kettle of fish for their own son to be contemplating that kind of move, particularly when he appeared to be doing well in moving up the corporate ladder. As a parent now, I understand their reservations. Abernethy's credibility had not really been established and could their son really make a useful contribution to a developing Christian ministry?

It wasn't long, however, until they recognised our confidence in God's leading and a genuine certainty in our hearts that this was clearly the right way forward for our lives. Since then, both sets of parents have been 100% behind our involvement in this exciting work. As parents and mentors, they have had an outstanding influence on so many of the things which God has accomplished with Abernethy over the years.

Move to Nethybridge
My contract with Thames Valley Newspapers concluded in September of that year and it was with tremendous anticipation that we drove up the M6, following a large furniture van towards Nethybridge, in search of the next phase of God's adventure for our lives. We experienced a great surge of peace about our new challenge, but would we be in a position to ride that wave for very long? There was so much to do and so little time to do it.

As we prayed and contemplated our move to Nethybridge, both of us had become aware of a growing confidence that our decision to get involved with Abernethy had been prompted by God. Neither of us had seen specific 'writing on the wall', no 'texts jumping out of the Bible', no ' I have a word for you' elders, but simply a real sense of peace in our hearts that we were going to be doing what God had planned for us. The training, work experience, Christian service opportunities and personality make-up all seemed to be fitting together to suit his ends. What a relief and what a privilege!

By this time we had two children—Sheona aged 3 and Findlay aged 1. We were delighted that they would be brought up in a rural setting although we were also aware of the potential dangers of institutionalised living. From the early days we tried to maintain a semblance of separate family life. It was not always easy as Centre pressures constantly tried to squeeze out family interests. Our family has been very patient and understanding although, at times, it obviously got to them. 'No talk of Centre things,' Sheona aged 10 would firmly say at teatime as Moira and I began heatedly to debate why the guests' meal was late or the central heating had broken down again. Sheona was so right!

As those early hectic years of Centre life eased off slightly, offspring number three came along in the form of Kirsty. There is no question, I made a better dad third time round—although Kirsty may not agree! Each of our children has played a very important part in our calling. As well as giving us so much fulfilment, happiness and sheer pleasure, they have also contributed to Centre life. From important tasks such as helping in the wash-up or serving in the shop, to instructing activities or taking part in an evening epilogue programme, each has played their part in the Team effort. We thank God for all three of them.

The early days were very tough but I wouldn't swop them for anything. Days were spent in painting and decorating, repairing and rebuilding, equipping and planning, marketing and selling, praying and begging. Finances were very scarce. A heavy overdraft held back any developments and a shortage of guests occupying the beds limited the potential of the work. The challenge was the potential for development and the clear purpose was to glorify God and make disciples for him, using the programme, staffing and the Centre as the vehicle for doing that. If we could improve the facilities, increase the guest occupancy and upgrade the programme, then we would manage to solve the financial difficulties and achieve our objective. And so with a small team of four or five, we set about the task in 1975 of achieving the overarching goals for the work of Abernethy.

At first we needed to fill the beds. Based in the Spey Valley, Scotland's major ski resort, it was obvious that a Christian outdoor centre ought to be offering ski courses. That meant qualified ski instructors and specialist equipment. Moira, myself and Iain Smith, our first chief instructor, set about getting ourselves professionally qualified. Our ski mentor was Dougie Godlington—an outstanding communicator of ski technique, knowledge and folklore. We all tried to copy his graceful style but sadly, without his success. Not only was he our skiing hero and our much-appreciated training mentor, but he has become a close friend of the Trust family, having helped us in a variety of ways throughout the four seasons of the year.

Other activities needed similar training to provide professional outdoor programmes. New facilities were required to meet the expectations of a growing market. Additional staff were recruited to meet the increased usage and appropriate administrative mechanisms installed to handle the extra business. They were exciting days as we experienced God's hand on the venture, directing and encouraging us step by step.

From the very beginning, Norman Walker's vision was to establish a Christian outdoor centre that was of a high standard, reflecting the quality of the message emanating from it. In my capacity as leader of the work, I have attempted to dispel the belief, held by many for far too long, that Christian organisations provide second-rate services and facilities. We adopted the slogan, 'Striving for Excellence in Christian Centre Outreach' in an attempt to underline that message. It is an ongoing battle but worth fighting for, because everything we do, good or bad, speaks very clearly about the Lord and Saviour we serve. That adds an important impetus to our efforts.

Of, course, it wasn't always easy. It seemed as if the Evil One knew exactly when to hit us and he did it by getting at different members of the Team, and each Centre (there are now several of them) has proved that time and time again over the years. Very often, problems have started through people being over-tired, a word wrongly spoken, a gossiped piece of news or a selfish act. Within a Christian community, things boil up very quickly, resulting in an apparent victory for Satan and an obvious diminishing of Christian outreach. If there is one particular gift which I crave more than any other it is the gift of wisdom and discernment in knowing how best to handle all the potential people problems that might arise within our Teams. Not that they are any greater or more frequent than in any other business, either Christian or secular. However, if they are allowed to develop, they can cause so much damage and the curtailment of the evangelistic activity of the team.

In each Centre, we have established an informal structure of leadership and supervision which helps alleviate some of the inevitable interpersonal relationship difficulties. Sometimes people think that Christian communities should be heaven on earth and in one sense, of course, they are; but the realities of living and working together in a Christian ministry do not take away from the fact that underneath we are all very human and susceptible to pressure and temptation. The Trust team is like a big family and, like all families, we have our ups and downs, good times and bad, joys and sorrows, times of closeness and periods of testing. Thankfully we are surrounded by a large host of God's troops protecting and guarding us as we serve him.

Other centres open

The Abernethy Trust has had many heroes over its first quarter-century. In fact, everyone who has served in any capacity to help move the work forward is, in my book, a hero because we wouldn't be where we are today were it not for the Christian men, women and young people who have contributed to the advancing momentum of this exciting Christian ministry. Some stand out in my memory because they have not only influenced the work, but have had a profound effect on my own involvement.

Peter and Margaret Jones arrived one morning in 1976. Whilst living in Australia, God had given them a special vision some three years before that they should travel across the world and get involved in setting up a

Christian ski lodge in Scotland. Here we were sitting in the front lounge at Abernethy discussing how God had brought them to us. We needed a painter with joinery skills. Peter did both. We needed a cook and a qualified nurse. Margaret was both. Most of all, we needed two more keen Christian people called by God into this expanding ministry. Within a few years of their arrival, God had unexpectedly presented us with Centre number Two on the island of Arran. Peter and Margaret were trained and ready to take on the job of leading the work there. In 1981, they travelled down with their young family to establish Abernethy's first offspring Centre in the village of Shiskine, on the island of Arran off the west coast of Scotland.

Richard Yarrow was another of my friends and heroes. He joined us at Abernethy as a ski instructor and very quickly demonstrated that he had leadership skills and management ability. When Peter went off to Arran, Richard took over the reins of his job and established himself as my deputy at Abernethy. He was a good all-rounder, skiing at a high standard, able in the mountains and very capable in running the administration. Richard helped to establish professional standards and was a powerful influence in people coming to know Jesus Christ for themselves. Very sadly, at the age of 34, he developed a brain tumour and died in 1987, leaving his wife, Sheila, and two sons. His memory is very real.

Relationships are an inevitable consequence of providing a vehicle for Christian service where young people of both sexes are likely to meet and work together. Over the last twenty years almost fifty couples have met and married as a result of being part of one of the Abernethy teams. Stamp collecting is not one of my hobbies, but I have, over the years, gathered together a portfolio of wedding photographs reminding me of all the new Christian families that have been established as a result of the Abernethy story.

Phil and Rosemary Simpson are part of that elite club. Both of them worked as team members back in the '70's—Rosemary as part of the catering department and Phil as a temporary summer instructor. Neither of them, I know, thought at the time that a few years down the road they would have completed their degrees, fallen in love, married each other and returned to the Trust, ready to take on the big leadership responsibility of Trust Centre number Three at Ardeonaig which opened in 1984. I had the thrill and privilege of performing their marriage ceremony in a small chapel in Norfolk. As a couple, and like so many others within the Trust, God has used their availability and obedience to him to achieve his purposes.

I am reminded of another Philip in Acts 8. He, like many of those early Christians, simply appeared to be wholly available for whatever God wanted him to do. It strikes me there is a key there to unlocking the secret of knowing God's will.

Hundreds of people have formed personal relationships with Jesus Christ since Abernethy was established and I could fill a book with their stories alone. Barney's story is a cracker and reads like a spiritual 'Mills and Boon'. I first met him on the ski slopes during a very snowy blizzard. It was one of those special conversations that immediately went below the surface of normal mundane matters. Before I knew it, he was telling me all about his past and particularly his search for answers and the real purpose of life. The minibuses, full of young people, waited patiently as we conversed together, oblivious of the appalling weather conditions around us, totally engrossed in our subject!

Gifted as a communicator and naturally musical, he was constantly in demand. For a while, teaching satisfied his expectations, but the sudden death of his first wife Iona only months after they were married, created a void and disillusionment with life. His four-year search for meaning culminated in leaving primary school teaching to set up a ski school in Tomintoul, close to the new Lecht ski area. In his own words, Barney would often say, 'Ski instructing has a high pose value and produces strong street cred. I like to think it had a kind of magnetic attraction for the ladies too. You could always spot the ski instructor during the height of the summer—he was the one walking around town still wearing his ski instructor's uniform even though the sweat was pouring off him.'

It was clear Barney was going nowhere fast and in his heart he knew it. Almost without his realising it, onto his ski scene at the Lecht came another group of ski instructors who seemed, for some reason, to be different. One particular female instructor had not escaped his notice. 'What's different about them and what's her name?' went through his mind. The pursuit and investigation had begun. Weeks later, as I stood there that day in the snow, privileged to be sharing my faith with a man desperately needing Jesus Christ to fill the gap in his empty existence, I realised that this was what a 'calling' is all about. Most of the time, it is just being available to allow God to use you as and when he wants.

Some months later, on Easter Sunday, Barney sat in my office with his elusive female instructor, Julie, and took his first faltering steps of asking Jesus to become his Saviour and Friend. It wasn't long before he joined us as a member of the Team. His relationship with Julie grew and developed and I was honoured to conduct their wedding service in the Walker Lounge at Abernethy. After a series of internal promotions over the following years, he and Julie with their two children, were in 1991 invited and commissioned to lead the development of the Trust's fourth Centre at Ardgour. Julie and Barney are two special people with whom I have had the privilege of growing and developing as a Christian leader, tackling together with them many of the challenging issues facing Christians today. They are a further illustration to me of how friends become mentors and mentors become friends in God's work.

Looking back at God's leading over the last thirty years has been much easier than it has been looking forward to see his plans. How fortunate I have been to have had so many perceptive mentors, patient friends and valuable super-heroes. As I have grown 'longer in the tooth', my own contribution to the work has appropriately changed as others have taken on responsibility. My role has adjusted to being one of an enabler, counsellor and, as some would even unkindly suggest, 'the Godfather'!

However, I still cherish my mentors and friends. Bruce Smith, now the chairman of the Abernethy Board, is one of my current role models. Not only do I value his close friendship, but greatly benefit from his wise counsel and balanced spiritual leadership. Surrounded by so many men and women of his calibre, partnered by my wife and best friend, Moira, and supported by my friends and mentors of the past, my ultimate Hero, Jesus himself, is constantly challenging me to make myself fully available and obedient for whatever he has for me in the years ahead.

The challenge is open to allcomers—even you.

3

FROM COTTAGE TO CASTLE

Neil Innes

In the quiet little hamlet of Knockfarrel in the Scottish Highlands, sheep could be heard bleeting, cattle lowing, birds singing, and in the rough grassy fields and slopes leading up to the crest of the hill, rabbits played. From our vantage point on the hillside, a tiny crofter's cottage was clearly visible in the centre of the picture.

It was in this little cottage on 10th October, 1936 that the cries of a newborn baby could be heard competing with the lowing cattle through the wall in the byre next door. Neil McMillan Douglas Innes had announced his arrival. Now, 58 years on from that date, I can look back at those early days and the years which followed with gratitude to God for the path which he had mapped out for me.

Country upbringing
Living in this crofting community was an idyllic experience. Idyllic indeed; no running water came from our taps, for there were no taps. One of my earliest chores was to draw buckets of water from the well! No supermarkets dominated our shopping; there wasn't even a corner shop from which to buy! No electricity lit up our evenings; oil lamps were the order of the night! No leisure centre or swimming pool was available to occupy

our spare time; we spent our evenings reading books or playing table games. Our link with the outside world came through a small battery-operated radio into which we tuned for the news bulletin morning and evening. Television wasn't thought of! Most significantly of all, our days began and ended with a reading from the Bible.

Our diet was very basic; salt herrings excited our taste buds and we were into organic food before that concept was ever dreamt of. We grew our own potatoes and vegetables, kept a cow who faithfully provided the daily milk from the cream of which butter was made. In addition to drawing water from the well, as a young lad I was also responsible for cleaning the byre in which the cow lived. I was growing up in what was indeed a 'green' environment!

In the community at nearby Lochussie, we were fortunate to have a primary school, where I began my education. Sadly governments of that day were also into the business of cutbacks. During my time at Lochussie, changes were made to the curriculum necessitating the completion of my primary education at nearby Maryburgh. No doubt many in the locality were disturbed by the changes and the eventual closure of the school, but for us children, living in a community without any form of public transport, it was an exciting prospect to have a taxi or bus ride to school each day. My secondary education was carried out at Dingwall Academy. School was never something I enjoyed and I cannot recollect excelling in any subject. I only pray that what a teacher was reported to have said about me is in fact true, 'I believe he is a better preacher than he was a mathematician!'

71

During my period at Dingwall Academy, I was introduced to Scripture Union and to the practice of reading for oneself a daily portion of the Bible. It was also at this time that I came into contact with an organisation called SASRA (The Soldiers' and Airmen's Scripture Readers Association). The then Scottish Representative of SASRA, Robert Stephen, came to visit my mother. That evening Mother and I walked the eight miles to Dingwall Gospel Hall and back, to hear our first account of Forces' evangelism. That began for me a friendship with Mr Stephen and later his wife who were to become affectionately known as Uncle Robert and Aunty 'B'. They were to prove a great influence for good and for God in my life. The report we heard made a deep impression on me. However, I remember declaring to Mother as we walked across the moors, 'I'm not going into the army. When the King sends for me (National Service), I am just not going.' Little did I realise that I would spend the greater part of my life working amongst soldiers and airmen.

The nearest centres of population to Knockfarrel were Strathpeffer, Dingwall and Maryburgh, all of which were about three to four miles away. It was to these places we went in order to shop or avail ourselves of any of the amenities available at that time. Although Maryburgh was the nearest location, we lived under the ancient Scottish parish system in the parish of Fodderty and our local church was considered to be in Strathpeffer.

Religious heritage
Reference has already been made to the daily practice of family worship in the home, at which time a metrical

psalm would be read and sung, a portion of Scripture read and prayer offered. That was very much part of the culture of the day. In addition, regular attendance at public worship was something that was required and expected in my home. Each week, I would regularly walk at least sixteen miles in order to sit under the preaching of the gospel and would also attend Sunday School in the little school at Lochussie. This meant that weekly, in order to achieve this religious observance, we walked some twenty miles.

At the time, I found it all very tedious. There was no bright hymn or chorus singing in our church, we sang only from the metrical psalms. No organ or piano accompanied the praise. This was the task of the Precentor or Song Leader. The address or sermon regularly lasted a minimum of 45 minutes. Sermonettes were unheard of! Great emphasis was placed in the home, at church and also in day school, on the practice of memorising Scripture and the Shorter Catechism. My mother came from a Free Church family but my stepfather was a Free Presbyterian, so I often found myself between the two. I would always opt for the Free Church because the sermons were shorter!

I was taken to the annual Scottish Northern Convention at Strathpeffer from an early age by my mother. I recall the preaching of well known Keswick Convention speakers who came and ministered God's Word, among them 'Fraser of Tain', a godly eccentric who had a remarkable ministry in his day. It was however the preaching of the Rev G B Duncan at the Convention in 1953 which made a deep impression on me.

Meeting with Christ

As I now record something of the crisis experience that finally brought me to faith in Christ, it is with the realisation that all that had gone before was part of God's gracious plan to make himself real to me.

On the face of it, I led a fairly upright life as a youngster, when I was found in the company of Christians more frequently than most of my age. Indeed, because of the outward veneer, there might have been many times when I would have passed as a Christian. That was the outward appearance but, inwardly, I was in a mess. Deceit, dishonesty, unbelief, envy, jealousy, greed, to mention but a few of the characteristics of the human heart, were rife in my life. I had religion but I did not have Jesus Christ. As the Holy Spirit drew me into a living relationship with Christ, he used all that had gone before and finally the gift of an evangelist in the ministry of the late Rev W R MacKay, the minister at that time of Kingussie Free Church.

Mr MacKay came to Strathpeffer in 1954 to conduct a week of evangelistic meetings. I was invited to attend by a godly aunt of my mother's. On the Wednesday evening, I left the church in a state of turmoil. Suddenly I sensed the awesomeness of God's Presence and the reality of my guilt. I spent a sleepless night as I tossed and turned. The battle for my soul was on! The enemy was real as he sowed seeds of unbelief and questions of doubt.

Morning came! At that time I was employed as an engineer's assistant on the Hydro Electric Schemes in Wester Ross. I thought, 'A good hard day's work will sort this out.' It didn't! Thursday night and Friday night were spent in the same way as the Holy Spirit convicted me of sin. At 5 am on Saturday, I opened the attic window of my bedroom and looked out on a beautiful sunrise. I remembered the Psalmist's words in Psalm 19:1: 'The heavens declare the glory of God; and the firmament showeth his handiwork' (AV).

Returning to the evangelistic meetings on Saturday night, I heard Mr MacKay preach from Revelation 22:17: 'And the Spirit and the bride say, Come. And let him that heareth say, Come. And let him that is athirst come. And whosoever will, let him take the water of life freely' (AV). During the service four young men gave their testimonies. All spoke of the reality of Christ having replaced religion in their experience. During the preaching God met with me in a very real way and I began to feel a sense of peace, as the clouds of conviction were blown away by the wind of the Spirit.

At the end of the service, Aunty Katie suggested that I go to the vestry to talk and pray with Mr MacKay and one of the elders, Alex Ross. This I did and left the church sensing the peace of God in my soul. As I journeyed home I asked myself the question, 'How do I know this is real?' Mr MacKay had pointed out to me that we are saved by grace through faith, not by feelings. I knew it was real when the Bible was read at family devotions. The book that had been so dead and boring to me was now the living Word of God.

Called to evangelise

My new found faith was nurtured by the faithful ministry of the Rev A G Ross. I will always be indebted to him and his wife for the way they cared for me, providing me with much needed Christian fellowship. Witnessing at work was not easy but I was encouraged to make my stand by the Church of Scotland Industrial Chaplain. The visits of the Highways & Byways Mission of the Free Church gave me the opportunity to witness in the open air. It was in the Prayer Meeting in Strathpeffer that I gave my first address, choosing as my text John 9:25: 'Whether he be a sinner or no, I know not. One thing I know, that, whereas I was blind, now I see' (AV).

The visit of a team from WEC (Worldwide Evangelisation Crusade) Missionary Training College in 1955 was a time of real challenge. After being involved with these young men, I was called to the work of an evangelist, following a missionary meeting. Responding to the challenge of God's Word and his Spirit, I reasoned with God as I cycled home. I could cycle no further. Abandoning my cycle at the roadside, I sat down on a rock in the grass verge and surrendered my life to Christ for service. Then, thumbing through my Bible before restarting my journey home, God spoke to me so clearly from 2 Timothy 4:2,5: 'Preach the word; be instant in season, out of season; reprove, rebuke, exhort with all longsuffering and doctrine ... But watch thou in all things, endure afflictions, do the work of an evangelist, make full proof of thy ministry' (AV). To this place of call I have resorted many times over the years. How thankful I am that God gave me this experience.

Such a clear call required an immediate response. I was joined by a fellow Christian, Mr Murdo Morison, who had a similar vision. On Friday evenings we would meet for prayer and then do personal evangelism in the streets outside the dance halls in Ross-shire. In some locations, we were able to obtain permission to preach the gospel to the revellers during the dance band break. Many were challenged and several of those who were leaders and organisers have since come to faith in Christ. We were not without criticism; some felt we were 'casting pearls before swine'. The motive of our hearts however was simple and sincere, to make Christ known.

Having attended a WEC Missionary Conference at Aberfoyle in 1955, I returned home to start the Dingwall Prayer Battery for WEC Missionaries worldwide. We met in the Dingwall Gospel Hall as an interdenominational group of Christians with a burden and vision for world evangelisation.

1955 was the year of Billy Graham's 'All Scotland Crusade' in the Kelvin Hall, Glasgow. Invited by a Church of Scotland Minister, Rev Malcolm Laing of Alness, I helped organise a chartered train to convey people from the Highlands to Glasgow. Amongst those who were invited by a friend and I to come, were a retired Indian Army Colonel, his wife and sister. All three came and professed faith in Christ along with many others.

For me that journey was my first south of Inverness. I was privileged to visit the crusade office with Mr Laing and met Dr Graham briefly. Later in the crusade, Dr Graham and the team came to Inverness where once again I was privileged to be invited by Mr Laing to have tea with them at the Palace Hotel. In the enthusiasm and excitement of the occasion, I invited Billy Graham to a round of golf at Strathpeffer, which, sadly for me, he had to decline!

These meetings were tremendously encouraging for me as a young man. The clarity and simplicity of Dr

Graham's presentation of the gospel is something that has remained with me throughout my ministry. Little did I realise that some 36 years later, I would be involved with a group of church leaders who invited Dr Graham to return to Scotland for Mission Scotland 1991. Indeed, the first consultation in Edinburgh took place in our home. Following that consultation, I took a daring step of faith. Believing it to be the Lord's will that Dr Graham should come to Edinburgh, I negotiated the reservation of Murrayfield Stadium before there was any confirmation of his coming. The Lord did indeed guide, for had that reservation not been placed, an alternative event would have occupied the stadium and Edinburgh would have been without a mission venue. It was my privilege to serve as a member of the Board and National Executive of Mission Scotland 91 and to coordinate the Livelink Mission.

Army service

It was only as I reflected at that point on 1955, that I realised the significance of my invitation to an army family to attend the Kelvin Hall. During 1954 and 1955, I faced the call of conscription to serve Queen and country for two years in the Armed Services. I recall so clearly the first set of call-up papers that came, inviting me to attend a medical board in Inverness. This I duly did and was told by the Medical Officer that I was unfit for military service, being underweight. In my heart there was a sense of that call to evangelism. Was God saying 'No National service for you?' I began to pray about Bible College Training. Twice more the same results were given. Perhaps God was going to give me the desire of my heart not to join the military. I applied to the Glasgow Bible Training Institute (now Glasgow Bible College) and to the WEC Missionary Training College, also then in Glasgow. Before a reply was received from either College, a fourth letter arrived from the War Office. Once again, I made the journey to Inverness, knowing that I had not put on an ounce in weight and expecting to be given the same report. To my astonishment, the same doctor who on three occasions had rejected me, now declared me fit for service subject to a satisfactory chest X-ray. I was stunned! What was God up to? Was I not sure he was guiding me to Bible College?

As I dressed in the cubicle of the examination room, I put my hand in my pocket and brought out a copy of the SGM (Scripture Gift Mission) booklet 'Daily Strength'. It was 12th January, 1956. The verses I read included those from Joshua 1:9: 'Have not I commanded you? Be strong and courageous. Do not be terrified; do not be discouraged, for the LORD your God will be with you wherever you go.' Would God be with me in this new situation? Yes, the assurance of his Word was real! Briefly, I bowed my head, gave thanks and asked for strength to stand. Later that day, the Lord afforded me the privilege of pointing a fellow-recruit to Christ.

Facing up to how a term of military service could fit in with a definite call to the work of evangelism was indeed a challenge. I began to feel that my call might be to the foreign field. Surely it would be wrong to waste two years of my life in the military! How could I redeem the time? After prayer, I decided to pursue the possibility of training as a nurse in the Royal Army Medical Corps (RAMC). This proved possible so it was arranged that in addition to my two years' National Service, I would sign on for another year, which in the end had to be extended to four in order to complete the SRN Course.

Finally, the day came when I had to leave my family in the Scottish Highlands to join the Army at Crookham, near Aldershot. Contact had been made with Robert Stephen of SASRA, advising him of my joining date. He gave the advice which I have passed on to many young Christians joining the military, 'Nail your colours to the mast on your first night in barracks. It will be tough but soon your comrades will respect you.'

When I reported at the Guard Room of the RAMC Depot, I was greeted by a rather loudmouthed Sergeant, who seemed more concerned about the length of my hair than he was to welcome me to the Depot. A very smartly-dressed soldier was instructed to take me to the training company accommodation. As we set out together, he seemed very tense and abrupt. Once out of sight of the Guard Room, he turned to me and said, 'Are you a believer?' How good our God is! 'In all your ways acknowledge him, and he will make your paths straight' (Proverbs 3:6). In just a few minutes' walk, I enjoyed fellowship with this fellow-Christian and was informed of all the Christian activities taking place on camp. He said, 'You have come to take my place. Tomorrow I am due for demob.'

'Nail your colours to the mast,' said Robert Stephen. How could I do this in a crowded Barrack Room? It took me a long time to find the courage to kneel by my bedside in the presence of my roommates. Finally I succeeded. The only reaction I received was from a rather vocal individual who had re-enlisted in the army. He claimed to be an atheist and sought to make a fool of me. He blasphemed and did everything he could to destroy my faith. Prayer was answered and eventually this individual came with me to hear the gospel at a SASRA meeting.

I will never forget my first encounter with a Scripture Reader. Within my first couple of days in the army, while sitting on my bed in a barrack room, the door opened and a uniformed gentleman stood in the entrance. We all stood up but were immediately told to relax. Then in a gentle but clear voice, he asked the question, 'Are there any Christians in this room?' Before I had a chance to respond, he said, 'I know there is at least one. Where is Neil Innes?' In the crowded room, Andrew Purslow greeted me as a Christian and welcomed me into the fellowship of SASRA. I was invited to the SASRA Meeting on camp that evening and then to Miss Daniels' Soldiers' Home in Aldershot when we were allowed to leave camp.

I will always thank God for the life and ministry of Andrew Purslow. He taught us so much about practical Christianity and what came through was his love for souls. During my time in the Depot, I met several whom he had led to Christ, among them the Sergeant-Major of the Apprentice College, Ken Sear, who, following a very successful career in the RAMC, retired from the army to become the General Secretary of SASRA (1981-1992).

One final reflection on these days in training will illustrate the hand of the Lord. Joe was a fellow-soldier who had become very depressed about service life; so much so that, on one occasion when I visited the platoon toilet block, I discovered him in an advanced state of preparations to take his own life. The Lord brought me to him at just the right moment. I was able to talk to him and take him to the Word of God. The Lord not only saved his life from physical death but also from spiritual death. My joy was complete when at my first SASRA 'Our Day' (Annual Meetings) in November, 1956, Joe was one of the many who shared his testimony to having found Christ during the year.

My basic training completed, I was posted to the British Military Hospital in Tidworth, Hampshire, to begin my SRN course. The Lord wonderfully enabled me in those days to come to grips with both the practical and theoretical sides of nursing. I was happy in this situation because I knew it was where God would have me be.

My first 48 hour-leave pass from hospital was spent with Christian friends in Acton, West London. I worshipped that weekend at Acton Green Railway Mission. The Lord's Day began with an early morning Prayer Meeting, at which I met an elderly gentleman named Mr Moules. He was a member of that fellowship and the preacher for the day. He invited me to share my testimony and a word from the Scriptures at the evening service. This I did, sharing a platform with that grand old man of God.

My second address was based on 1 Corinthians 12:27: 'Now ye are the body of Christ and members in particular.' As I prepared in the afternoon, the Lord showed me that I could illustrate the oneness of the body of Christ and the importance of each member from my anatomy and physiology lectures which I was in the midst of at the hospital. How important this message is and always will be. The Lord abhors divisions amongst his people. His cause is hindered and our spiritual lives are impoverished by failing to recognise Christ in each other and to lay aside the trivia of denominational differences in order to advance together the cause of Christ in the world.

I was invited by Mr Moules to return to Acton when next I had a weekend pass. That visit coincided with the arrival home of his son and daughter-in-law from missionary service in the Himalayas. God was pleased to bring me into contact with one of the greatest missionary statesmen this century. Thus began a friendship with the late Leonard C Moules and his dear wife Iris, who together did much to encourage and develop my potential for ministry.

Preparation for serving the Master
I was now beginning to appreciate that the fulfilment of the call God had given to me was being realised. The four years at the hospital were formative years, firstly under the guidance and counsel of ASR Albert Currell and then under the ministry of ASR Jim Kirk. Both of these men were faithful evangelists and able teachers of the Word. Little did I realise what God was up to. Earlier I mentioned my desire to enter Bible College. However, here in Tidworth, I was privileged to have a personal tutor in both of these godly men. They not only came alongside me personally to teach me the Scriptures but also allowed me to share in their evangelistic outreach and, in some small way, to begin to develop the gift of the evangelist that God had bestowed on me. I had embarked not on a two-year course of study but rather had

begun what, in the end, was nine years of personal and practical preparation for serving the Lord.

In 1957 I became the SASRA Branch Secretary (Fellowship Leader) in Tidworth and assumed leadership of the SASRA fellowship at the hospital. This appointment gave me the opportunity to meet Captain H S May at SASRA Headquarters. How we enjoyed receiving letters from him! These were always spiritually stimulating and full of good practical advice.

I recall that in my enthusiasm for the Lord, I approached a surgeon whom I had been told was a believer, as he was about to enter the operating theatre. He immediately cut me off. We served together at the hospital for some considerable time before having fellowship together. The telephone rang one day in the ward where I was working. The voice on the other end of the line said, 'Can you meet me tonight at the hospital chapel?' It was Captain Keith Buckler, the surgeon I have just mentioned. We met that evening on our knees, saying little to each other, but pouring our hearts out to the Lord as we confessed how wrong it had been for us not to have fellowship together. The Lord spoke to us from his word: 'All men will know that you are my disciples if you love one another' (John 13:35).

That evening, we agreed to meet daily at 6.30 am to pray, provided we were not on duty. What we witnessed over the following three months was quite remarkable. Some thirteen members of our Unit were won for the Lord Jesus Christ. The prayer-time that began with two of us grew to almost twenty on a regular basis. As we sought to lay aside our personal difference as Christians, we saw God at work in the lives of others. At one stage the barrack room in which I lived was home for fifteen individuals, out of which eight were committed Christians.

During my years at Tidworth, these are some of the lessons that I learned:

1. Walk in the light with your fellow believers.

2. Make prayer, personal Bible Study and Scripture memory priorities in your life.

3. Be aware of the need for life and lip to be in harmony in order to be an effective witness.

4. Build bridges of friendship to those around you and earn the right to witness to them.

All these were essential lessons for me to learn if I was going to be able to fulfil to the ultimate the call God had given me.

In 1959, I completed and successfully passed my State Registered Nurse qualifications and, soon afterwards, I was posted to a Field Ambulance to take part in a major military exercise in the North African Desert. In this situation also, the Lord was very precious. An outing to the town of Cyrene afforded me the opportunity to share the gospel with my section, as I read to them from Matthew 27:27-56 where we are told about the soldiers who compelled Simon, a citizen of this town, to bear the cross of Jesus.

It is important that we take the needed steps to prepare to obey the call that God has given; preparation time can be useful time, as the Lord confirms the gifts he has given. At this point in my career, I had no green light from the Lord to leave the services; so I extended my engagement, initially for six and then for nine years.

The remaining years of my military service were

spent on the staff of the RAMC Depot where I began my service, then in the Army Careers Office in Glasgow, and finally at the Junior Tradesmen's Regiment in Rhyl in North Wales. It was the years between 1961 and 1964 in Glasgow that were to be for me the final stage of preparation for full-time Christian service. Working on the Army Careers Staff enabled me to go on several courses which allowed me to develop communication skills. Spiritually, I was greatly helped by a number of individual Christians and church fellowships, in particular Grant Street Free Church, Harper Memorial Baptist Church and Eastpark Gospel Hall. Involvement with a team conducting an open air meeting in Sauchiehall Street further developed my preaching and personal evangelism skills. In 1963, I was instrumental in arranging a mission which this team conducted in Ross-shire, my home county. Some 43 individuals professed faith in Christ at that time.

I was fortunate to be stationed close to the SASRA Scottish Office and my lunch breaks were usually spent there in the company of Mr Robert Stephen and his secretary Mrs Pearl McGibbon. Robert Stephen did much to encourage my zeal for the Lord, affording me opportunities to witness at SASRA deputation meetings and latterly, during this period, he put many preaching appointments across my way.

Barbara

While stationed in Glasgow, the Lord brought Barbara Mathieson Fraser into my life. Converted at St George's Tron Church under the ministry of the late Rev Tom Allan, Barbara worked as a secretary at the local Army

Headquarters in the city. We met for the first time one Saturday morning in Pickering and Inglis bookshop where she had a Saturday job. I had come from an all night prayer meeting for the open air work into the shop to buy a commentary. The friendship that began that day blossomed into a romance, the result of which was our marriage by Mr Robert Stephen in East Park Gospel Hall on 18th August, 1964. The Lord had put in place a husband-and-wife team that, in less than twelve months time, would be engaged in full-time Christian service with SASRA.

The mission field to which God had called me was not some far-flung place across the other side of the world but the armed forces of our own nation. Barbara had felt called to serve the Lord perhaps in the Far East or South East Asia but, in a wonderful way, the Lord confirmed the call into SASRA. During my final unit in Rhyl, while on duty late one night as Orderly Sergeant, God spoke to me from the call of Abraham (Genesis 12) and confirmed my call into the work of SASRA. You can imagine my thrill and amazement on returning home the next day to find Barbara's Bible lying open at Genesis 12. How good God is! How essential it is to have the partner of God's choosing and, if called to embark on service for the Lord, that your partner shares the same conviction.

Working with SASRA
We applied to SASRA and were accepted as full-time workers from 1st July 1965. SASRA is a missionary organisation, recognised by the Ministry of Defence, with permission to carry out evangelism in Army and Royal Air Force units. They fulfil this ministry through

a team of evangelists called Scripture Readers, all of whom are ex-Service men and women.

My army service finished on 27th May 1965. At 6.10 am, I returned to Barbara at her parents' home where she had moved earlier, and at 6.11 pm on the same day our first child Rachel was born. Once again God's timing was perfect.

It was agreed that Barbara would remain with her parents while I went on training with SASRA. This training began on 1st July. I was to be attached to four full-time workers for a period of six months. The initial two months were spent in Germany with ASR John Findlay at Rheindahlen and ASR Frank Crofts at Bielefeld. What treasured memories I have of these days, as these experienced evangelists took me into their lives and graciously and gently taught me what and what not to do when seeking to win men and women for Christ. We have a watchword in our ministry. It is 1 Corinthians 2:2: 'For I resolved to know nothing while I was with you except Jesus Christ and him crucified.' This is summed up in the line of the hymn, 'To cry, behold the Lamb!' How blessed I was to have the privilege of pointing several to Christ in this first assignment!

Tested
The battle was however beginning to rage on another front. Throughout my years as a Christian, I have been very conscious of the enemy of men's souls, Satan himself. His objectives are to frustrate the preaching of the gospel and to destroy the testimony of the Christian worker, which he will endeavour to do in a variety of ways.

When I left for Germany, Barbara was unwell following the birth of Rachel. How our call was now to be tested! Weeks passed and there was no letter from home. International telephone calls were at a premium. Eventually I obtained permission to telephone from the officers' mess. Back home in Scotland Barbara was ill, Rachel was ill and Barbara's mother had suffered a severe stroke and was now hospitalised. I contacted SASRA HQ and the General Secretary informed me I should stay where I was and he would investigate the situation. I received a terse message, 'Remain where you are, we are praying.' What should I do? I was tempted to resign and return home. The truth of Romans 8:28 began to have real meaning. I was serving the Lord in obedience to his call and could trust him to take care of my ill wife and baby. How glad I am with hindsight that I stayed the course on that occasion. It was indeed a character-moulding experience. My remaining training assignments were with ASR Jim Kirk at Catterick Garrison and with ASR Bob White at RAF Lyneham.

Edinburgh

It was to Edinburgh Garrison that we were posted for our first appointment. Here too our faith would be tested. During our first night in the SASRA house, Barbara took ill and had to be admitted to hospital, where she spent her first two weeks of our stay in Edinburgh. This was followed three months later by a further crisis when her mother died following a second stroke. That was the traumatic beginning to what was to be a very challenging and fulfilling six years and ten months as the Garrison Scripture Reader in Edinburgh. Now I was to put to the

89

test all the Lord had been teaching me during the previous nine years.

1967 saw the launch of the SASRA Rest Room ministry at the Edinburgh Tattoo and our first links with the Gurkha soldiers from Nepal. Previously I had shared in a remarkable experience of reaching out to these men at Tidworth with ASR Jim Kirk in 1961. For Barbara, the Lord seemed to bring the reality of her call to the East together with our call to SASRA, as we reached these men for Christ. Helped by a missionary couple on furlough from Nepal and a blind Nepalese Christian, we saw three of these individuals turn from Hindu darkness to Jesus Christ. Only recently we had news of one of them who, after many years of persecution, has seen his wife converted. Since then there have been many other remarkable opportunities to reach and win these men for Christ. Even as these lines are being penned, we have welcomed five Gurkha Christians to our home.

I recall an evening in our Edinburgh home when it was full of young soldiers from the barracks. That evening I led two men to Christ. Little did I realise that, within a few weeks, both would be face to face with Christ, having lost their lives as a result of terrorist violence in Northern Ireland. This was one of three occasions when the Lord taught me the responsibility of the stewardship of the gospel placed on the evangelist. On two other occasions to my knowledge, within twelve hours of sharing the gospel with young men, they were ushered into eternity.

The way was often hard and the furrow that I was ploughing as a Scripture Reader was tough. We had many discouragements along the way, not least from

Christians who seemed keen to support and encourage, only to let you down a few days later. I was only able to continue in these difficult times through the encouragement of my wife and our ability to return to our place of call. During our time in Edinburgh, our family increased to three with the birth of Ruth in 1967 and Jonathan in 1971.

Germany

In October 1972, we left Edinburgh for a new challenge. We were posted to Bielefeld in West Germany to be attached to HQ 1(BR) Corps to replace our senior colleagues ASR Jim and May Kirk who came home to Edinburgh. Our youngest son Timothy was born in Germany in January 1973.

The work in Germany has, over the years, been slightly different from that in the UK because of the need to provide more Christian fellowship for believers.

Since 1952, SASRA had had an Easter Convention at which the Word of God was expounded and times of fellowship shared. Our arrival in Germany came at a time when the Services were becoming more and more composed of married men and therefore, with them, their families. The Easter Convention was geared for the single man. We took up the challenge, ended the run of Conventions in 1973, and began to pray that the Lord would show clearly the way ahead. In 1975, in an amazing way, he led us to commence the SASRA Easter Convention at Haus Stapelage, a conference that catered for the whole family. Since 1975 the Lord has blessed these gatherings and many have found the Saviour there.

In addition to the traditional work of Barrack Room

evangelism, in Germany Barbara and I developed a children's work and, through the Good News Clubs, families were reached and won for Christ. Regular visits were made to Berlin where, eventually, we were able to deploy another worker. As a result of the groundwork done with Chaplains in Germany, we were able to see a whole new area of work developed in the North East at Celle.

How quickly our time passed! In 1976, we returned to the United Kingdom.

Back to Britain

After nine months in Colchester, the SASRA council invited me to take over responsibility for Scotland, the Isle of Man and the Border Counties of England. The apprenticeship which I had served during those years in the Army in Glasgow with Mr Robert Stephen now fell into place. The Lord had entrusted to me the task his faithful servant was fulfilling when I first heard of SASRA at twelve years of age in 1948. How I valued his council in my early years as Scottish Representative!

In addition to personal evangelism, I was now engaged in a preaching ministry, as I shared the work and preached the gospel up and down the length and breadth of Scotland. Initially, we worked from Bishopbriggs, where Barbara was not only a faithful wife and mother but my efficient PA. We have always worked as a husband-and-wife-team and, without her support and encouragement, I could not have continued in the work.

In 1987 we moved our base with the Scottish office to Balerno near Edinburgh. This move enabled me to visit the Scottish Division Depot as a Scripture Reader following the withdrawal of our full-time worker, as a result of military cutbacks.

1988 was a very significant year in the history of SASRA, being its 150th Anniversary. This occasion was marked by a service of thanksgiving in the Guards' Chapel, Wellington Barracks, London, attended by our Royal Patron, Her Majesty The Queen. Following the service, both Barbara and I, along with our colleagues, were presented to Her Majesty. It was also a year in which our faith was further tested through Barbara's health when she was diagnosed as having breast cancer, necessitating mastectomy surgery. Once again we were thrust upon the Lord who alone is our strength and shield.

Our story began in that little crofter's cottage at Knockfarrel and this chapter must end in the Banqueting Hall of Edinburgh Castle where, on 8th October 1990, I was awarded the General Officer Commanding Scotland's Commendation for meritorious service to the Army. The citation acknowledged the work that Barbara and I had carried out together over twenty five years. We do not look for earthly recognition as we serve the King of Kings, but such recognition served to show us how much our work was appreciated by the powers that be. I recalled that day how in 1968, on a Saturday evening in a Rest Area at Edinburgh Castle, I had pointed a Gurkha soldier to Christ. My journey from cottage to castle has been truly worthwhile with the Lord as my constant companion and guide.

4

IN STEP WITH THE MASTER

Pauline Stableford

I suppose it all started with tears and a prayer on Easter Saturday 1960. There have been many tears and many prayers since then, tears of frustration, prayers in all sorts of moods. But those tears and that prayer were the basis for a whole new life.

Born into a loving but only nominally Christian family, I had been sent to a local Sunday School with my sisters. We learned Bible stories there, but were not challenged to make a personal commitment. It was not until I arrived at Nottingham University that I first heard the gospel clearly presented. I found it was not just a question of knowing the Bible stories, but responding to them. I asked Jesus into my life as my personal Saviour. Now the Bible I had known for years took on new meaning, and I found joy in a personal relationship with Jesus instead of impersonal knowledge about him.

For the rest of my time at university I grew in my faith, planning how I would be a good language teacher for Jesus. I didn't ask if this was his will, I just carried on with my own plans—I had always wanted to be a teacher. At university I was having problems with French literature, which I hated. Eventually I had to repeat some of my French exams in order to get my degree. So I spent a year at home, working and studying.

Looking for Christian fellowship over Easter I 'happened' across a Christian conference not far from my home. It was run by a mission I had never heard of before, the European Christian Mission, an international and interdenominational mission founded in Estonia in 1904.

God challenges me
The theme of the conference was 'Jesus is Lord'. I recall that the visiting speaker was the Rev Arthur Coffey, and I remember that he was quite humorous. But when he was speaking about putting your life on the altar for God I was really challenged. An invisible hand seemed to lift me to my feet, with tears streaming down my cheeks, as the invitation was given. But although God used a man in a meeting to challenge me, I had to talk it out with God alone, and escaped to my room as quickly as possible after the meeting. And there I was on my knees by my bed, weeping Pauline out and Jesus in to the 'driving seat' in my life. Only the Holy Spirit told me what to say, as I surrendered to him control over the three important areas of my life: marriage, money and career. Let me look at these separately in the light of the years that have passed since that day.

I never decided, as some people assume, not to marry. I decided to let Jesus have control of that question, and (so far!) he has not led me into marriage. I have not always found that easy, but then again I have sometimes been profoundly grateful for it. Mostly I have just got on with the job of serving God day by day, knowing he is in control. Looking back, I could never have been as mobile or as available for the work the Lord has given me if I had had a family.

Money has never been a big problem—living on 'peanuts' with Jesus in control has been quite adequate. Being brought up to look at every penny twice (even though we weren't Scottish!) I simply continued to do so. Of course I sometimes thought it would be nice to live more comfortably, eat out more often or buy fashionable new clothes. But those were wants, not needs, and do not add to the real quality of life. Basically, I do not have expensive tastes in food or entertainment, and I am willing to wear handed-down clothing. This has helped to stretch the pennies to cover all my needs. God has been a faithful Provider through various channels.

Giving my career to Jesus was, at the time, the most difficult. I had always wanted to be a teacher, preferably a language teacher. It was like putting Isaac on the altar to say I would give that up and go out to spread the gospel, which was what I felt the Lord was calling me to do. 'But if that is what you want, Lord, here I am. Use me if you can.' Looking back I see how the Lord took and blessed that offering and gave it back to me to use in his service. Both in language teaching and Bible teaching I have been able to use the gift he gave me for his glory.

Four things were clear in my mind as I rose from my knees that day: (1) all for Jesus; (2) full-time service; (3) Europe; (4) European Christian Mission. I hadn't heard any voice, but these things were imprinted on my mind. Apart from the first one, which was instant and irrevocable, it took time for the others to be fulfilled, and in more recent years those have been changed. I learned that the call to follow Jesus with all my heart and soul was the only unchanging criterion in life. He can change or develop the direction of his call as he wills.

PAULINE STABLEFORD

God leads to Finland

I applied to the Bible Training Institute in Glasgow (now known as Glasgow Bible College) but was only offered a place for the following year. So I went ahead with plans already laid, to spend a year teaching English in Finland. I had been looking for a post teaching abroad for a year, but could only find an opening in Finland, a country I knew nothing about. Later I learned that such teaching jobs are available in many countries, but the Lord obviously kept all those doors not only closed but out of sight. And so I ended up in this 'last choice' country, with which I soon fell in love. The first months went well and I enjoyed getting to know both the people and the country, not to mention the almost impossible language.

I was asked to inform the British Council in Helsinki by the end of December if I wanted to continue a second year. My reply was in the negative because I was thinking of going to Bible College. In February a chance remark hit me. 'Why don't you stay a second year?' asked my friend Anna. Should I? Could I? I wrote to Helsinki to ask if I could change my mind. Surely it would be impossible by now, but I prayed that if the Lord wanted me there longer, he would do the impossible. The reply came: Tomorrow would be too late, today you can! Then Anna said, 'Now you must decide.' I must decide? But I had asked God. I was thrown into a frenzy of uncertainty as I set off to walk home from Anna's place. Jesus walked beside me as I argued with him—'Lord, now I have to decide ...'. I seemed almost to hear a voice in my ear, 'You asked for an answer and I gave it.' 'Yes Lord, but ...'. 'You asked and I answered.' 'I know, but ...'. 'I gave you my answer.' By the time I reached home

I was convinced. I stayed and the Lord's reasons became clear with time.

I was able to postpone my Bible training for a year. When that second year had passed I returned as planned to Britain and travelled to Glasgow. After one happy year at the Bible Training Institute I spent the summer in Finland, speaking at ladies' days, tent meetings, etc. with my not-yet fluent Finnish. Although I had supposed I would be working in a German-speaking country because I spoke that language fluently, the thought began to grow about working in Finland. Again I asked the Lord to show me his will, not by specific sign, but just by opening or closing the door. I spoke to the director of the Church of Finland Inland Mission, which I had been working with all summer. 'Would there be a place for me in your mission?' 'Yes,' he replied encouragingly, 'I'm sure there would.' The door was open.

I bounced back to BTI with a cheery 'Guess what! The Lord is opening the door for me to work in Finland!' 'No surprise,' said my friends, 'you talk about Finland as if you belonged, so we reckoned the Lord would have to send you there!' Funny how other people sometimes see more than you do of the Lord's work in your life, isn't it? I have more than once found it helpful to have confirmation of God's directions through the witness of Christian friends. Yet it is equally important, if the guidance comes from outside, to have the confirmation within one's own heart.

By the time I returned to work in Finland the Lord had changed my attitude. Instead of being rather afraid to speak up for Jesus, that became my greatest joy. I began teaching English and German at the college of the Inland

Mission. Sometimes I went out to evangelistic campaigns with their workers, and I also worked actively amongst the students. Since the college was residential there were many opportunities to speak both publicly and privately about my Lord. Often I worked together with Raili, an equally enthusiastic Finnish girl of my own age. We visited the girls' dormitories to chat with them, and we organised testimony meetings round a blazing log fire on Saturday evenings.

In the spring came the question of continuing for another year there. I saw the alternative as moving into full-time evangelism with this mission. If I were to stay, then there must be fruit. This time I 'laid out a fleece' to God. 'If you still want me at this college, Lord, I need to lead ten students to know you this year.' By the end of the year I had knelt with only five to help them accept Jesus. It did not satisfy me that many others, affected by my testimony, had turned to my Finnish friend Raili for help in asking Jesus into their lives. I gave in my notice. When my friends told me this was a stupid thing to do, I tried to reverse it, but other arrangements had already been made. Moreover, there was no place free on the evangelistic team. I was in limbo! 'Lord, have I made a mistake? Or is this you showing me that when you give answers they are not reversible?'

On a visit to Helsinki a friend introduced me to the Bible School there, where they might need an English teacher. At my interview I promised that if the previous teacher didn't return I would take the position. But it included teaching at a kindergarten—a thought which horrified me. I have never prayed not to get a job like I did then! 'Please Lord, bring that girl back.' He didn't.

Although I enjoyed teaching the adult students, I hated the kindergarten. I am just not cut out for children's work. But knowing the Lord had put me there I determined to get to like it. It took a long struggle, but by the end of the year I could honestly say it was bearable and I had grown fond of the children. Certainly I had learnt a great deal about them and how to deal with them.

Then came the next test. Would I be willing to change my hours there, making the adult lessons a rush to get to? I prayed hard and eventually had to say 'Yes'. But then came the release. Helena, the only qualified kindergarten teacher, left, so we could only have it as a club once a week, and I was quite happy to run that with the help of my students. I am still not a children's worker, but would not be afraid to help out sometime. And I learned to obey the Lord, even when the task given was one I felt completely inadequate for.

I continued at the Bible School, teaching various subjects and supervising the student hostel. Contact with the European Christian Mission, which had almost been lost, was re-established, and I heard of their need for a representative in Scandinavia. By this time I had also started learning Swedish and realised this was a job I could and would love to do. In May 1968 I talked with Stuart Harris, the General Director, who was happy at the prospect. And yet I had no peace. I was standing in front of traffic lights, raring to go, but the red light was on.

I realised I wanted to run away from the difficulties at the Bible School. There were pressures from above and below. The director, although a very capable Bible teacher, was often unnecessarily hard on and critical of the staff, including me. Then there were rebellious students. As the school was a training college for work in Lutheran churches, not all the students were really committed Christians.

I remember one in particular, Eero. He was attending a general course at the Bible School, not the church worker course. But he lived in the hostel, where I upheld the rules laid down by the school directorate. These included 'No boys in the girls' half of the house after ten in the evening.' Eero didn't like this, feeling it was too restrictive. And he made me personally responsible for it. 'You are an old maid, and you don't want to marry, so you don't understand us young people who do,' was his accusation one day. This arrogant and incorrect statement was made to a mere 27-year old! But God didn't want me to run away from these difficulties, and I had to withdraw my application to the mission before I got peace in my heart. The following year was even more difficult, but I had the victory through obedience.

European Christian Mission representative in Scandinavia

When Mr Harris wrote six months later to ask whether I could now consider giving more time to ECM, his letter seemed to glow with God's green light. Before the end of term a new director for the Bible School was appointed, who promised me an easier life there and tried to persuade me not to leave. But I was going forwards now, not running away. I was following God's timing, and it felt good.

Building up European Christian Mission work from scratch, first in Finland, then all over Scandinavia, was certainly not easy. Locked into their denominations, people were not open to an interdenominational mission. They also regarded the whole of Europe as Christian, and not in need of missionaries. Have you ever felt you were hitting your head against a brick wall?

It would have been easy to give up, but God didn't make me that way. He gave me a large portion of what the Finns call 'sisu'—stickability. Used for one's own purposes this can translate as 'obstinacy' but latched on to God's purposes it means 'tenacity', hanging in there to see his goals achieved.

It was only many years later that I saw the extent of the impression my work had made. Markus, a pastor in the denomination of which I was a member, said to me not long ago: 'When you first came and started talking about Europe we thought you were mad. But you never gave up. You kept on telling us, and eventually the light dawned.' Yes, the brick wall had given way rather than my head! This denomination has been supporting work in Europe for some years now. God had sent others to work to the same end at the same time in different ways, so the effect was greater. Today it is well accepted by most Christians in Scandinavia that Europe is a mission field.

The loneliness of the work, both in the office and travelling all over Scandinavia to present Europe in many different churches, eventually took its toll, and after eleven years I felt in need of some sort of change. *Administration* was the word that dropped into my head, 'out of the blue'. What, how, where? Is this my idea or the Lord's? I couldn't see any possibilities and nearly dismissed the thought. Then I went to ECM prayer days in Austria, where the European Director, Jack Murray, spoke of his need of administrative help in the office in Germany. My knees felt weak. Afterwards he came over to me and said, 'I was thinking of you. Are you interested?' 'Yes!' I replied at once, realising this was what the Lord was preparing me for with that simple word from 'the blue'. How important it is to be tuned in to God's wavelength so we can hear his promptings, even if we don't understand them at first! He will explain what he means if we are listening carefully and prayerfully.

Move to Germany
It was quite a pull to move from Scandinavia (I was by that time living in Sweden to be more centrally located for my travels), after a total of more than 18 years there. My responsibilities included keeping in touch with and sometimes visiting those countries, so contact was certainly not lost. By this time my home church in Helsinki (I had no home church in Britain) had started supporting me, which they have faithfully continued to do. The German language and culture were familiar to me from years before, but obviously I needed readjustment after the years up north.

I enjoyed the new challenge and the team work instead of working on my own. However, full-time office work was in the long run not my thing, and in the third year I was happy the Lord opened up the possibility of part-time work with the local free church of which I had become a member. I visited several ladies, encouraging them and doing regular Bible study with them.

In spring 1984 an opportunity opened up to work full-time in a small evangelical church in the very north of Germany. The influx of about forty new Christians after a tent campaign was too much for the five members to cope with. I moved up there at the same time as Johann, a young pastor straight from seminary, arrived with his wife Annette, and together we set about the privileged job of discipling these people.

We had our ups and downs, there were joys and disappointments, sometimes personal relationships had to be struggled through, talked over, forgiven. Annette and I had different ideas about certain things because of our different ages and backgrounds. Occasionally we clashed, but with a talk, sometimes with tears, we could forgive each other and eventually became the best of friends. We saw and felt the devil attacking our fellowship, but we rejoiced too in the One who has the victory over him.

It was some time at the beginning of my third year there that I felt suddenly detached from the situation, as if the soil was being loosened around my 'roots'. I always try to thrust down roots as soon as possible in a new place. We all need to belong, and this is the way I feel I belong somewhere. On several occasions preceding a move the Lord has 'loosened the soil', even when I had no idea when or what he wanted to move me to. So this time too, I did not know what he had in mind, but realised my time at that job was drawing to a close. I kept the knowledge to myself and prayed as I continued with the work in hand.

Tentmaker in the Far East
An idea began to develop in my heart about returning to teaching English for a while. I had done some research on 'tentmaker ministries' whilst in the European Chris-

tian Mission office in southern Germany, and the idea began to appeal to me. But where? A missionary newsletter arrived on my desk. The front page shouted that English teachers were needed for the Far East. I smiled and put it aside, took it out, wrote for further information, and put it away again. That was not for me! Finland! I'll go back there to teach until I see the way further ahead. I wrote to the appropriate address, and found there was a place available almost immediately in an ideally situated town. 'Thank you Lord, this looks perfect.' I applied by return post.

No answer came for some time. Eventually I phoned. 'Oh, we had appointed somebody else by the time your application arrived' was the off-hand answer. Slam! Ow! 'Lord, that hurt!' I am not sure to this day why that little episode occurred. Maybe I was pushing too hard at the door I wanted to go through. Maybe the Lord wanted to show the contrast with where I eventually ended up, where he could still keep me and where I was certainly more needed. But I do know the Lord never hurts us without a purpose.

By this time I had received more information on the Far East, although I still did not seriously suppose the Lord would send me there. Europe was my mission field, always had been, always would be! At nearly 50 I was certainly not thinking of uprooting myself to another continent. But God was!

He had spoken in various quiet ways before, but this time he knew he would have to shout loud and clear if I was to hear. It was through a Trans World Radio broadcast late one evening that the Lord eventually shouted the name of my new country at me. It was not to be mistaken, as it came three times in the context of a missionary call, and it was not to be denied. 'Alright Lord, you win, I'll go. Hallelujah!'

My application was accepted, though eyebrows were raised at one statement. In answer to the question, 'What do you hope personally to get out of this time in the Far East?' most people apparently spoke of new experiences, professional furtherment, etc. I had replied, 'I am not looking for personal advantage, I am coming in simple obedience to God's command.' It was the plain truth. Why should it be so unusual as to cause raised eyebrows? Are we even expected to do Christian work with a view to personal profit?

No placing was available for autumn 1987, so I agreed to start with language study, leaving open the possibility of a job turning up if God so wanted. He did. A message came to say a new college had been found that was looking for a single lady in her forties. 'You are the only one on our list fitting that description' I was told, so I agreed to go. (The previous male teacher had got drunk and been fresh with the girl students, hence this stipulation.) I didn't know it then, but this confirmation not only of the land but also of the exact place was going to be a great help to get me through the difficulties of the first year.

I could have given up a dozen times—the electricity was more often off than on, so I never knew when I could cook; the place was extremely primitive so that even the students complained; the water was polluted, giving me a skin rash; I got shingles; my mother died in faraway Britain; the summer was too hot and the winter too cold, without air-conditioning or heating; I was constantly fighting a losing battle with mice and mosquitoes; I had no fellowship except with two other teachers at weekends. The list is endless, but each problem was surmountable because I knew with certainty that I was in the right place, and that Jesus was with me. At that point I couldn't tell people that, and my life had to be my sermon until the Lord gave suitable opportunities to share my faith in words. Several people came to know the Lord during that year.

One door closes but another opens
I expected to stay on longer, the university had said they wanted me. Our director came to visit, asking if I knew of anyone to fill a further new place they had been offered. He went to visit my university's leaders and came back with the shock news that they didn't want me after all. They had their excuses, of course, but later we understood it was because of my Christian witness.

However, the next door was already there wide open—isn't God amazing! So I moved on to a more civilised, more comfortable life with clean water and no mice or electricity cuts. It felt like luxury, though you wouldn't have thought so if you had come straight from Britain. There I was without any fellowship for a year other than with an occasional visitor. But there were those who needed, through my life and eventually my words, to hear for the first time of the One who loves them. As a few came to accept Jesus as their Saviour we began a small fellowship, which was a help to me as well as to them during the two years I spent at that college.

I have said earlier, that the Lord usually 'loosened the soil' before he moved me on. This time he didn't.

After the summer holiday in Europe it came like a bombshell—work permit will not be renewed. The reasons were obvious—I had been warned regularly during the last term not to talk about 'religion' to the students.

For about two years after that I experienced no direct guidance, no loud voices, no green lights. I helped out in an office for several months and then returned to Britain to plans that never worked out. I got to know the feeling of rejection when job applications were unsuccessful, but at the same time warm acceptance by folk in a local church. The Lord had not changed and he had not fallen permanently silent. I shall see the meaning of this period in my life, as of all other periods, when the whole patchwork picture is revealed in heaven. God can lead us quietly in the everyday common sense decisions of life. We can find useful work for the Lord even when 'unemployed' by taking every day as a gift to live for him.

It was during my second year in Britain that Hungary came into the picture, through hearing two bits of information about it. Rather than a suspicion (that the Lord's hand was in this) followed by a 'click' of assurance, this time it was a 'click' to start with followed by prayer to confirm it.

The confirmation just grew unspectacularly, helped along by a reconnoitring visit and then an invitation to help with work amongst the migrant Asians there. An unexpected development came as I was asked to teach at an international Bible Institute, and this work is proving both interesting and challenging. At the time of writing there are unexpected developments in the migrant work. I am having to look for new approaches and opportunities to reach the unreached with the Good News of God's forgiving love. In all of this I am trying to keep my ear attuned to the Lord's leading as I go step by step.

God of small details
I have mostly recounted how the Lord led me in big matters, questions of where I should live, what I should do. During my years in Scandinavia I was also involved in visiting Eastern Europe, then still under communist domination. Here it was a question of being led in the smallest details as we visited people, carried Bibles, and sought to minister to the suffering church without causing them any problems with the authorities.

One week in particular stands out in my memory. God was guiding me every step of the way. Taina, who only spoke Finnish, came as a 'silent partner' to help with the driving and pray whilst I did the talking. It was my first visit to Poland and I had no names or addresses, only a clear inner conviction that I should go. I also had a load of Russian Bibles and some clothes. The friends in Sweden who had got the Bibles for us did not ask where we were going. But they offered us some Hungarian Bibles they had tried to send by post, but which had just been returned. I turned them down, not seeing any use for them. However, as we sat in the car saying goodbye, I suddenly felt I should take them. So I sent the daughter to fetch them and tucked them under my seat.

At the border the car in front of us was searched thoroughly. We prayed. When it came to us we pointed to our camping gear on the roof and were waved through! We hardly touched the road the first few miles, and never had a skylark sounded so sweet when we stopped for a rest! The first evening we stopped at a campsite, where we found some Swedish young people. I had a feeling they could be Christians, but didn't like to ask—one just didn't ask that sort of question, even of Swedes, in the middle of a communist country. So, using my 'sanctified imagination' (a close cousin of sanctified common sense), I sang a Christian song in Swedish just loud enough to be heard from my tent to theirs. When we later met in the kitchen the contact was made. Yes, they were Christians, and they were able to give us some church addresses from a booklet they had.

Armed with this information we drove into the capital, Warsaw, during a thunder storm. As soon as the rain stopped I got out and asked for the street we wanted. 'First right and right again' I was told. And there we were—God had led us through the storm to exactly the right place in this large city. That church was happy to take half the clothing and the Bibles, which they would be delighted to pass on.

Some of their young folk took us to the home of Mary, a dear sister, who happened to know ECM. We turned out to be an answer to her prayer to get a letter out to the West. During our conversation I cautiously asked whether she had any contact with Hungary. Equally cautiously she said she had a little. 'Why do you ask?' 'Well,' I replied slowly, 'I have a few Hungarian Bibles with me.' 'Hallelujah!' Mary cried, leaping up with joy. 'We have some Hungarian friends coming tomorrow and I had prayed the Lord would send us some Bibles to give them.' Yes, God had seen the need, heard the prayer, and answered through someone who had no idea about that, but who was willing to listen to God's voice.

From there two girls guided us to their home town and

sent word round to friends to gather at church, where I was asked to speak. What should I say? I prayed and flipped through a small notebook for ideas. Some brief notes made from a sermon on the Holy Spirit caught my eye, and I used those. The young people afterwards thanked me, saying they knew so little about the Holy Spirit and that my talk was really helpful. Surely the Lord knew that in advance.

With further addresses given to us we continued to another town and were asked to bring greetings at the Baptist Church there. Because there was a lady who could interpret from German rather than English I used that language to share something of the Lord's love and about our common faith. I wasn't quite sure what I had said to make two old ladies weep, so I asked them afterwards. It turned out they were German-speaking and were so moved to hear God's word in their own language after so many years. How beautifully the Lord works to bless his humble children.

As we made our way home from that visit we could hardly believe we had done so much in one week. We had visited nine homes and spoken in three churches, apart from delivering our precious cargo of Bibles and clothes into eager hands, and all this without any previous arrangements, names or addresses. The Lord proved at every step that he was in control as we obeyed his leading.

'Put the radio in your bag, and those last two Bibles,' Anne ordered as we got out of the car. 'I think we might need them here.' We had identified the house we wanted as we drove past, and were now parked some distance away. We were in Rumania, in winter this time, and had been given this address by friends. We only knew that the brother we were to visit had been in prison for translating Christian books into his language.

Brother Tom welcomed us with open arms and we chatted for some time. Then I asked, 'Do you listen to Trans World Radio programmes?'

'Many people do here, and they are very helpful,' he replied. 'But I gave my radio away many years ago and I haven't the money to buy another.'

'Would you listen if you had one?' I asked, my fingers itching on the handle of the bag holding the radio God had led us to put into it.

Tom gave a sad smile. 'My sister is old and getting blind, so she can't come to church with us. It would be wonderful for her to listen. But ...' he shrugged his shoulders, 'There is just no way I can buy one.'

By this time the bag was open and I was pulling out the radio. I put it on the table in front of him. 'Now you have one,' I said simply.

At first, Brother Tom was completely taken aback, then his eyes lit up, his face glowed. 'It's a miracle!' he breathed quietly, then repeated it more loudly. 'It's a miracle!' He looked up at us with tears in his eyes and began to explain: 'Two days ago I began to pray for a radio for my sister. No-one knows about this, not even my sister. I have never had such a quick answer to prayer.'

We laughed together and praised God together. The sister came in and he told her the news. She was delighted. But she also saw I had put two books on the table. The feel of them told her they were Bibles. 'Oh, isn't God good!' she exclaimed. 'We gave away our last extra Bible this morning, and already he has replaced it with two more.' Yes, God is indeed good. Two unsuspecting missionaries had been able to bring joy and blessing to these dear people by being willing to follow his leading in detail.

'Lord, please give us fine weather, so that we can make this long drive safely.' This was our prayer as we continued our journey from Tom's home. But the Lord knew better. This is an important point to remember when asking for guidance. We sometimes ask for it according to what we think will be best, like asking for fine weather on that occasion. Anne and I were in an area where tourists rarely went, and where a foreign car could easily be spotted. We needed cover, and God gave it in the form of snow. Not only did it probably disguise our number plates, but it meant the few people who had to be out on the street had coat collars turned up and eyes on the ground instead of on us.

We arrived at our destination at midnight and had to wake people up to deliver our precious gifts. It was safer that way. After a brief time of praise with our brothers and sisters there we left, trying to put as many miles as possible between us and them before daylight. But petrol was running out. 'Lord,' we breathed, 'if we get stranded on the road here in the mountains, questions will be asked that we would rather not answer.' 'Do you think there will be petrol stations open overnight?' Anne asked. 'Don't be silly!' was my inapt reply, 'Be glad there are some that are open in the daytime.'

We drove into a small town before dawn, having been unable to sleep in the cold car. 'I daren't go any further, we'll have to wait here until they open,' said Anne as she drove into a petrol station we spotted. We had hardly turned the engine off when a sleepy attendant came out rubbing his eyes and filled our tank with no questions asked! We drove on in amazement and with thanks to our Great Jehovah for guiding us in such detail.

Listening to God's voice

Looking back I see some times when the Lord's voice has been clear, other times when it has been quiet and needed listening for. I see the clue to the ability to hear his voice at all in the complete surrender I recounted at the beginning. If we are listening for God's voice, wanting to know his will in order to decide whether or not to do it, we may well listen in vain. To the heart that has already said its unconditional 'Yes!' to God's will, he is much more ready to reveal that will. Yes, there may be fights over the harder moments—'Lord, you don't really want me to do that, do you?'— Jesus had one of those moments in Gethsemane. But the eventual submission is much easier if the principle has been established that I want to do God's will, even when it is hard.

One of those moments for me came during a missionary meeting in recent years. Although the area and work being spoken about were near my heart, the mission represented was, for certain reasons, right off my list of favourites! Suddenly a little voice inside me said, 'Give a thousand pounds to that project.' 'What?' I countered, 'that much? and to them? No way!' My limited nest-egg from savings and my parents' legacy was too precious to give to a mission I was not too friendly towards. I sat uncomfortably through the rest of the meeting, realising it was God's voice and if I squashed it I was putting myself into danger. Refusing to listen to God when he speaks clearly is not only a sin, it also means I am less likely to hear him next time. It wasn't worth it. I paid up with a smile, thanking God that he obviously did not share my prejudice.

There is a skin-friendly and ecology-friendly washing powder in Finland called 'Mini Risk'. I love to learn from everyday things around us, the kind of things from which Jesus drew lessons. That washing powder immediately reminded me that our Christianity is so often of the mini-risk variety. We want to follow Jesus if it will not be too uncomfortable, if it doesn't cost too much, if it won't spoil our reputation amongst neighbours or colleagues, or if it will enhance our career prospects.

When we put God's will first in our lives, as Jesus did, we enter the 'maxi-risk' area, where comparatively few dare to tread. Businessmen who work on the big risk principle may become rich, or may go broke. The maxi-risk Christian life will invariably lead to increasing inward riches, although outwardly we may well experience suffering and difficulties, and even poverty. Following the Master at all costs is an adventure in itself, a maxi-risk, maxi-blessing adventure, not to be missed.

This has been my experience so far. I don't expect to experience otherwise in the future, because Jesus is my unchanging, faithful Saviour. At the Bible Training Institute our theme song was 'Great is Thy Faithfulness'. When I sing that hymn today my eyes fill with tears of gratitude, because it is still so true. Although I have failed him many times, my Lord has never once failed me. Through many struggles, joys and sorrows, as I have put my hand in his, he has led me all the way. 'Great is Thy Faithfulness!'

5

ALL THAT JESUS SAID AND DID

Paul Harvey

We are 'chosen in Christ before the foundation of the world'. Our formation in the womb is known by God from eternity. He watches over us and guards our footsteps before ever we sense his presence. And yet I can remember no clearly spiritual experience in my childhood.

I was born in 1946 and my infancy was spent in Cannock, Staffordshire. We moved to Gloucester in 1954, where my father had secured a teaching post in a secondary school.

I succeeded in 'Eleven Plus', to my mild surprise, and was therefore able to go to Grammar School. The overall effect of the Sixties on me was quite disruptive. My academic progress eventually foundered while I was at college and I left a degree course in chemistry halfway through.

Jobs were easy to find in 1967, so at the age of 21 I started work with Richard, Thomas and Baldwin, the Welsh steel company, at their research establishment near Aylesbury. Within a year the whole business had moved to Port Talbot under the aegis of the revived British Steel Corporation.

One of the staff in the new department was John Isaac. I was warned by those who knew him that he was 'very religious' and would not be amused by dirty jokes or swearing. John was not a central figure in my life, but his strange evangelical convictions were interesting and sometimes infuriating.

In 1970 I married Helen, who had twin daughters. We settled in Llanelli. In due time I became the twins' adoptive father. In addition to my daytime job with British Steel I ran a successful mobile 'disco' business which took me away from home several evenings a week. The strain of this absence upon family life was considerable, but I stubbornly refused to give it up. I was enjoying it too much.

In the following five years, a series of events, divinely ordained, hedged me around and broke down my strongholds. God showed me that I was not the master of my own destiny. He made me teachable. I began to respond to John Isaac's oft-repeated invitations to hear the gospel.

Receive new life
In December 1975, at a Carol Service held by the Christian Fellowship in Port Talbot Works, I heard the Voice that raises the dead to life. I entered the family of God as a newborn babe. The new life in me demanded spiritual food and I found that the church where John Isaac was a member satisfied my new appetite for spiritual knowledge.

Bethel Church in Gorseinon was blessed with a godly pastor and many faithful members. At the Sunday services and the midweek meetings the gospel was preached and the great truths of Scripture were taught with unusual power. At some of the prayer meetings the occasional visitor would declare that revival had come to

Bethel. I do not think that it was full-fledged revival, but God did indeed come very close to us on several occasions. Without previous experience I assumed it was the norm of church life. I have discovered in the years since that it was extraordinary. I long to see it, and better, again!

The more of this atmosphere I experienced, the greater my desire to know God became. I started to read the Bible, using Murray McCheyne's plan which enables a reading of the entire Old Testament once a year and the New Testament and Psalms twice a year, at the rate of four chapters a day. It is a plan I heartily recommend, because over the years it builds a formidable foundation of Bible knowledge.

I was enjoying the effects of a changed heart. Almost unwittingly I had developed an obedience to godly promptings. It was not a human determination to change my sinful ways that motivated me; it was the effect of a new love. The Spirit of Christ was implanted in me.

After a few weeks of dreamlike happiness among my new friends I remember waking one morning with a cold feeling of 'reality'. I felt I had been living in a fool's paradise. It was time to snap out of it and take things more seriously. I could not expect my new-found God to do everything for me. If I carried on in this irresponsible way, there could only be disaster.

This unwelcome train of thought disturbed me because it seemed so depressingly realistic. I had begun to think that God would carry me and be my helper. Now I reasoned that he wanted me to take responsibility. He sent me out to fight and win life's battles and return to him victorious for his 'Well done!'

Make restitution for past wrongs

Another chill 'reality' began to intrude on my happiness. Now that I knew right from wrong, I must put right the wrongs I had done. I could not allow a conscience of past misdeeds to cloud my relationship with God. I delved back through my past. What offences had I caused? What had I stolen?

I surprised a librarian by returning books that I had removed from the library without his knowledge. I told him why I was doing it and he thanked me for being so honest. I attempted to trace a dentist whom I defrauded of fees for treatment. I had to give up my search for him, which left me ungratified.

Other, older crimes came to mind. Some of them involved the guilt of other people. I became burdened with anxiety. If I could not clear my record without injuring others, what was I to do? When I read the Bible or prayed, always my thoughts would return to my dilemma.

In desperation I went to the pastor for advice. It took courage, for I feared he would confirm my thoughts and press me to continue. He was not in, but his wife asked if she could help. She listened graciously as I explained my problem and she shrugged non-committally. If I felt that I must pursue my old crimes and clear them, then so be it. God would not allow me to be the loser in it. It was not the answer I wanted. It offered me no clear path of action.

I returned to the dilemma. Absent-mindedly I opened the Bible again in order to find help. I read in Exodus of the miraculous walk through the Red Sea and envied the Israelites because they had seen God's power to deliver them dramatically from their enemies. Then I read that they woke the morning after and went down to the beach. I pictured them as they kicked at the lifeless bodies of Egyptian soldiers washed up on the sand.

Suddenly the truth of the story hit me. Their old enemies no longer had any power over them. I understood instantly the parallel with my old life and past sins. I had been tricked by our spiritual enemy of souls. He had persuaded me that they still had power to spoil my communion with my Lord. Now God showed me that they had no power. They were history. I could not forget them, but they were dead to me, as I was to them. I could not, nor did I wish to, return to them, any more than the Israelites could, or would, walk back over the Red Sea to Egypt.

My heart leapt with relief and gratitude. The effect on me has been permanent. From that moment on I understood the power of the death of Christ to deliver me from sin and of his blood to wash me clean of the stains in my old life.

I learnt an important lesson in that early experience. God alone can answer the deepest anxieties of the heart effectually. We do well not to usurp his authority in this. We must be determined to lead the needy person to develop a deeper relationship with God, however often we have to point the way. The unhealthy alternative is a human reliance on the strength of the counsellor's character.

What to do with the disco business?
The disco business was thriving. I was 'resident' disc jockey in a Gorseinon night club. The manager of the

club was sympathetic to the revolution which was going on in my life and allowed me on Thursday nights to go first to the Bible Study in Bethel Church before I began the night's work in the Club! What strange days those were! In the breaks, when I was off-stage, I would rush up to the dressing room and spend half-an-hour avidly reading Watchman Nee's *Normal Christian Life* or Oswald Smith's *The Man God Uses*.

All the staff in the Club knew what had happened to me. Some mocked, one or two were seriously interested and even came to church with me once or twice, but without lasting results.

The break with that particular vestige of my old life came when I was obliged as compére to introduce on stage for a few nights a cabaret artiste who is better known for his TV family shows. In contrast to his sticky-sweet television manner, his cabaret show is blasphemous and obscene. The audience howled with mirth during his act, while I sat embarrassed and miserable.

For the first time I faced the inadvisability of continuing to work in such an environment. I saw clearly that it was not possible to partition that part of my life from the rest. I resolved to leave the disco business, much as I loved it, because to stay would dishonour my new Master.

Helen was opposed to my resigning. I was perplexed. The disco business had a destructive effect on our relationship because I was out so often. I assumed she would be pleased to see it go. But she protested that without the income from the business we would be struggling to make ends meet. She prophesied financial ruin, but I could see no alternative. Whatever the consequences, I had to resign. I played my last night at the club and sold the records and the equipment. The last record I ever played was 'The Old Rugged Cross'. It was a talking point for some weeks afterwards among the club-goers.

Older members of Bethel Church congratulated me on my decision and confided that they had been praying for that very thing for months! I was surprised. They had never once lectured me on the sinfulness of my night life. They were content to see God work his way in me.

Financial ruin nearly did strike us, in accordance with Helen's prophecy and entirely because of my tendency to procrastinate.

I had registered the start of the disco business with the Inland Revenue so that everything was above board. What I had not done was keep the books properly during the two-and-a-half years of business. Eventually, after numerous reminders, the Revenue Office sent me an estimated bill for unpaid taxes of around £3000! Naturally I had not one tenth of that sum to my name.

In a state of panic I took my small sheaf of receipts and cheque stubs to an accountant. He reassured me that the Revenue's actions were designed to have that effect on me and that I should leave it to him. Unbelievably, I allowed the matter to lie unresolved again for several months, despite the urgency to settle the account.

I remember one night attempting to push the matter out of my mind. Oh, the foolishness of procrastination! I looked to the Bible for encouragement. I was reading Romans 13, in line with McCheyne's plan for the day. Verse 6 said 'Pay taxes'! The very thing I was trying to ignore had been pushed back under my nose by my best Friend! Yet still I refused to act!

The Revenue office eventually sent me a summons. Again I ran to my accountant who with great patience plodded with me through the books. When the muddle was sorted out, it transpired that for most of the period of business I made no significant profit, and for the last most successful year I owed a reasonable amount of tax, which I paid with relief and gratitude.

I am amazed now at my stupidity. Why did I not act promptly? It would have saved me so much apprehension and a few nasty shocks. I learnt, however, from the experience to address difficulties immediately. If they are left, they fester.

Marriage break-up

Though I had now released more time for family life, Helen's unhappiness grew steadily. She seemed to want to spend more and more time away from the house. Her growing involvement in work and leisure activities sometimes meant long periods away from home, but she loved it.

I reacted badly at the start. I wanted her with me. The thought that she was away 'having fun' made me angry, and as soon as she returned I would reprove her for neglecting her family. Predictably she sought diversions even more strenuously.

I recognised eventually what I was doing. I saw from Scripture that Christ loved his Church unconditionally and that Paul taught that husbands should love their wives as Christ loved the Church. I began to apply the teaching. Rather than complain about her absences when she returned, I behaved in a way that told her it was lovely to have her back.

Nevertheless it became clear that Helen no longer wished to sustain our marriage. She filed for divorce in 1980 on the grounds that I was 'not the man she married' and that my personality change had cause an 'irretrievable breakdown' in the marriage. In her own way she was right. The change in me was irreversible and beyond my control. From her point of view my character was becoming steadily less attractive.

Divorce is an inescapably unpleasant business. I was mortified at the loss of her love. I did not know how to respond to the divorce petition. How would I present a defence? I realised that divorce proceedings could become a bitter round of accusations. I did not want that; it would not be seemly. But I did not want to lose Helen. I loved her.

I realised that this decision could not be made for me. I must discern the right way and walk in it. I read the instructions from Paul to the Corinthians concerning the conduct of believers towards their unbelieving partners. I decided that I should not offer a defence. 'If the unbeliever leaves, let it be so. A believer is not bound in such circumstances; God has called us to peace' (1 Corinthians 7:15).

The decree absolute was granted in November 1980, much to my grief and to the perplexity of many who were praying. We all thought that God would intervene in some marvellous way to prevent it.

Helen left the family home and moved into a rented cottage. The children stayed with her at weekends and returned for school during the week.

'Family life' settled into its altered pattern. What a strange situation! I had lost my wife and was now obliged to live with her mother in order to maintain a family to which Helen could return if she wished. This arrangement continued for two years, but as the children grew it became clear that I should live elsewhere. Helen had moved to her own house and the twins were quite happy to live with her. There was no problem in allowing me access to see them as often as I wished.

So, in the Autumn of 1982, I left the 'family home' and with very few earthly possessions, moved to share a rented house with a fellow member of Bethel Church.

Learning to live again
My father and mother, who in all these events were unwaveringly supportive, told me afterwards that they regarded this as the lowest point of my life. At the age of 36, what had I to show? My marriage was finished, I had no home to call my own, and I was reduced to a bachelor existence more usually seen in the life of a student.

Human loneliness is a terrible thing. I felt it acutely during this period in my life. I had good Christian company of course and the friendship of my colleagues at work. But my experiences could not be shared by them. I had to live them through with the Lord only as my Companion and Guide. It was in such times that my knowledge of him deepened the most.

I decided that I should buy my own house in Gorseinon. Mum and Dad were helpful in providing the initial finance for the purchase and I moved in to a newly refurbished two-bedroom house in the Spring of 1983.

My father said something prophetic at the time. As soon as he uttered the words, I recognised a divine authority behind them and I clung to it in the ensuing years. He simply said, 'This is a turning point in your life, son. Things will get much better from now on.'

The house was a wonderful little place, warm and secure. It took me a long time to get used to the idea that it was meant for me. It was not borrowed. I was there on nobody's sufferance. I kept it as I wanted to, came and went as I wished. Bethel Church was a short walk away and there was a dependable daily lift to Port Talbot for work. I was able to settle into a routine which suited me.

I entered a tight financial period. My bank account was chronically overdrawn and I was constantly anxious about money. I began to wonder whether I would have to leave my lovely little house and find a cheaper way to live.

I applied for a job as a Sales Representative in South Wales for a large pharmaceutical company. Although it was the first job interview I had tried since 1968, I did so well that I got on to the short list. I felt encouraged by this, feeling that it was perhaps the Lord's doing, yet still unsure of whether I was right to proceed. The second interview also went well and as I waited for the letter which would tell me of success or failure, I tried to decide what I would do if I was offered the job.

In such a frame of mind I was walking deep in thought at work, and as I passed one of the workshop fitters, he handed me a buckle. 'Here, take it,' he said. 'I found it outside in the gutter and polished it up. You might as well have it,' and off he walked. I looked down at it. It was a belt buckle, cast from brass, bearing the name 'Jerusalem'! I showed my Christian colleagues in work. They were puzzled. It was certainly a strange thing, but what did it mean?

That evening there was the usual prayer meeting in Bethel at which we specifically prayed for revival. It was customary afterwards to sit together and share something of what we had read or experienced during the week. I produced my buckle. I asked the pastor for some help in understanding what it meant in the light of my wish to change jobs. He was reluctant at first to tell me what he felt I should already have deduced. Well, maybe I had, but I did not want to face the facts.

'It appears simple to me,' he said. 'Do not leave Jerusalem, but wait for the gift—the Holy Spirit (Acts 1:4). God has had to present you with a tangible message to stay where you are!'

I knew he was right, but it was like a voice of doom. I went home most miserable. I sat in the dark for ages arguing with God, yet always came back to the plain evidence of the buckle. Miserably I admitted defeat. 'Not my will but yours,' whatever the consequences. I felt ashamed that I had got so far on my own path and asked the Lord to help me walk the right way. After all, he knew my problems.

I resolved to refuse the job if it was offered. God is gracious. I received a letter of rejection. He spared me the agony of refusing the offer.

From that point onward there was no immediate, dramatic deliverance. I did not inherit a fortune the next day. But little by little things began to improve and my finances returned to an even keel.

In 1984, four years after divorcing me, Helen remarried. Life is not inevitably filled with happy endings for a Christian. God has such high purposes for us and his desire to sanctify us is paramount. Thus he acts in ways that sometimes defy our comprehension in order to refine us. I understood this. I could see the divine principle. But I still felt the pain. One cannot always rejoice at the heavenly discipline that must be applied to an earthly life.

Searching for meaning

I now asked myself the question, 'Was the dissolution of the marriage designed by God to free me for some special work?'

I used to attend missionary meetings held by WEC (Worldwide Evangelisation Crusade) which always concluded with an invitation to stand during the closing prayer as a declaration of willingness to serve God in whatever way he chose. At one such meeting I stood, simply to signify that I was open to his leading. It took courage, because I had no idea what the call could mean. David Davies, the WEC secretary in South Wales, took note of me and came to offer his blessing.

Despite this, there was no clear leading for me to enter full-time work. I did not wish to enter any sort of 'trial period' of voluntary work. My reading of the biographies of missionaries and pastors led me to conclude that their calling was clear and inescapable. There was never any mention of a trial period. I concluded that the Lord did not intend me to leave secular employment.

My life entered a period of uneventfulness which lasted four years. I look back now with very little memory of the flow of events. There was little else but the daily trip to work, keeping my house clean and tidy, and attending the various meetings at Bethel.

Nevertheless, a sense of loneliness sometimes overtook me and I battled grimly to surrender to God's purposes. I would enter into a debate with him about the 'unfairness' of my experience. What had I done to deserve it? Why should I be alone?

'Battling to surrender' is a paradox that other Christians will recognise. It is Gethsemane. One draws close to the heart of the Lord Jesus at such times.

I remember the moment of final surrender quite clearly. It happened late in 1987, halfway down the stairs in my house. Between one tread and the next I resolved to leave the future in the Lord's hands. I had attempted to do so before, but somehow had never felt that the matter was closed. On that occasion I knew with relief that the battle was finally over.

I was unaware that somebody else in the Bethel fellowship had faced the same battle crisis at the same time and had experienced the same finality of surrender. We were both unaware that we would soon be married.

Marion
In 1977, Marion Eldridge had moved from the Midlands to Pontardulais, about five miles from Gorseinon, with her husband Peter and two boys, Philip and David. They had made Bethel their spiritual home and were a fine asset to the fellowship.

Peter and Marion used to invite me occasionally to spend a Sunday afternoon with them and I appreciated Peter's gentle but thorough way of bringing out the important matters in our discussions about how I was 'getting on'. They were enduring hard times themselves. Peter had been made redundant in 1981 at the age 46, but despite their own problems they always had time for me.

Peter eventually secured a permanent job again in 1985 and it appeared that the family had emerged from their long experience of hardship. Then, early in 1986, Peter developed symptoms first thought to be hepatitis and then diagnosed as liver cancer. He died in April of that year. Marion was left as a young widow with their two boys. She was obliged to work full-time, run the household and be mother and father to her children. Her own account of those tragic years is full of experience of God's lovingkindness.

The beauty of her character was admired by all. She was always thoughtful and loving. It would have been easy for her to descend into a pit of despair under the circumstances. She could have justified bitterness and thrived on selfishness. None of these things was seen in her.

Sometimes she felt her own loneliness acutely. She asked the Lord unanswerable questions such as, 'Why me? Why have all these things happened to us?' Was she to bring up her boys, to be left alone when they grew up?

She wrestled to rest in God's will, just as I had. And in the same way the victory finally came in the briefest of moments. She read one morning the words, 'I have learned to be content whatever the circumstances' (Philippians 4:11), and the whole matter was settled in that instant. She left her future in God's care and understood the foolishness of continuing to ask 'Why?'

Once the Lord had brought us both independently to quiet submission, he started to work very quickly to bring us together. There are times in the experience of believers when the Lord works in providence at a dizzying speed, and we were entering such a period. To our mutual delight we found that our friendship was deepening into love and we began to consider the possibility of marriage.

A new location

In the Autumn of 1988 I was offered a new job. The new post was in Havant, Hampshire, working for a company which supplied British Steel with paints. It was a natural progression in career terms. I was eminently qualified for the work, and would advance fittingly in seniority and salary. If I stayed in British Steel it was quite likely that I would remain in the same grade doing the same work until I retired.

Some of my Christian friends and even my colleagues at work reminded me of 'The Buckle'. Had not God made it very clear then that he wished me to stay exactly where I was? I concluded that the buckle was a dramatic tangible message for that moment of crisis. I had it still in my possession. (I have it still.) It would never 'evaporate'. It was a landmark in my history, but I could not allow it to become a stumbling-block in my life.

As Marion and I considered our future together, underpinning all our thinking was a growing conviction that, whatever misgivings we may have about the opportunity now presented, the Lord was opening the way to marriage and the move to Hampshire. It had his stamp on it.

At the end of December 1988 I said goodbye to Welsh Laboratories and closed a 20-year chapter in my career. I sold my little house, quickly and easily, to my parents, who had decided to move back to Britain permanently from Spain. I bought a car, my first for six years, and moved down to Havant to begin work with Hydro.

I experienced a mixture of emotions as I travelled, one of which I have discovered is common to anyone who makes a radical change in life.

I had checked into the hotel on Hayling Island where I was to stay temporarily. The receptionist had taken me to my room, which was comfortable, and wished me a pleasant stay. As she closed the door and left me alone I was suddenly overwhelmed with bleakness and isolation. I said to myself, 'What have I done? I've burned my bridges, left a secure job, a house and familiar surroundings—for an uncertain future!'

I have found that others, Christians and otherwise, have experienced the same emotion under the same circumstances. It is part of our psychology to regard the familiar as secure and to feel an irrational panic when we leave that security, however logical and sensible the change may be. It is transient and has no bearing on our actual situation.

Marion and I were married in May 1990, to the delight of our families and our friends. It was a wonderful day. My daughters were Marion's maids-in-waiting, her two boys 'gave her away' and my father was my 'best man'.

We felt that it was the close of a dark and fearsome chapter in our lives. One of the presiding ministers, Brynmor Jones, read this passage from the Song of Songs:

'Arise, my darling and come with me.
The winter is past. Flowers appear on the earth;
The season of singing has come ... ' (2:10-12).

Brynmor spoke to us in the presence of the congregation and expressed his conviction that these sacred words were meant for us. His sentiments echoed in our hearts. We heard a gracious Voice behind Brynmor's words. God had brought us into a time of tranquillity and wished us to share it joyfully together in matrimony. Brynmor's brief address that day scattered the last vestiges of gloomy thoughts from our minds. He confirmed for us that all we had experienced together, all we had felt for each other, was right and good.

Once married, our strategy in finding a house was simple. First we chose a church in Chichester, about ten miles from Havant, then looked for a house within walking distance of it. Chichester Baptist Church had godly leaders and a fine membership. We felt almost immediately at home among such lovely people.

We quickly became involved in the life of the fellowship and made some good friends among the members, which helped Marion greatly in adjusting to the move. She felt the loss of her friends in South Wales very deeply. Women put down much deeper roots than men.

Church involvement

The ministry and atmosphere of the Chichester church was dramatically different from that of Bethel. The change did us good. There were house-groups for Bible study—a movement discouraged in South Wales—from which we gained much. The benefits of the house-group in developing personal relationships with other church members far outweighed any supposed tendency to encourage factions within the fellowship.

The Sunday services were more free in worship than

we were used to. There was no excess, no contrived 'invocation' of the Spirit's presence, but the worshippers knew that the Lord heard them and that his heart was gladdened.

I was obliged to revise my view of God's Church. I discovered that there was Life in England! I realised that I had become more than a little spiritually xenophobic in South Wales.

As our roots deepened in Chichester we grew to love the area and the people. We were recruited into the Covenanters work in the Church, which drew us very close to the children in our care and to their parents. Marion taught the little ones in the 'Starters' group and I had a difficult class of 'Juco' boys.

For the first few Sundays with those lads, I wondered whether I should give up. One or two of them were extremely disruptive and appeared to take no notice of me. Much prayer was offered and I persevered. Bonds of affection began to grow with the most difficult boys. By the time I left the work, they were for the most part teachable and showed evidence of the working of grace in them.

It was while I was teaching them, preparing weekly lesson material, that I discovered they enjoyed simple Bible exposition in the much-maligned old-fashioned way, sometimes called the 'Guru-Devotee' method, rather than the 'induction' method now favoured by educationalists.

I have since found that young people are tired of the 'induction' approach. They are also weary of discussions which begin with a social issue and end with the Biblical answer. I strongly recommend a return to Bible exposition for young minds. They need to know the authoritative teaching of the Bible, and to observe humanity in the light of the knowledge.

We had difficulty in selling Marion's house in South Wales. The housing market had just entered its long decline and only one or two people showed any interest in it. Hydro had kindly supplied a bridging loan which we confidently expected to be able to discharge within the six months granted. The house was still not sold when the time expired and Hydro extended the period of grace another three months.

We both experienced times of deep anxiety immediately on waking in the mornings. Our sleep was not disturbed, but the moment we awoke, dark thoughts filled our minds. One morning, I was lying in the first minutes of wakefulness, battling again with unanswerable questions about how we would manage financially if the bridging loan were withdrawn before the house was sold.

Suddenly I wondered how these thoughts arose. They did not occur at any other time. When I was fully awake and immersed in the day's activities the problem did not concern me much. We had trusted God to undertake for the unsold house and were content to leave the problem to him. There was nothing we could do about it.

Why then did we have such a struggle in the early morning? I remembered what somebody had written about the Lord's temptations in the wilderness. The suggestions with which the Devil attacked him were designed to bring about his fall. It was the trial of 'the last Adam', when he was weak with hunger. The same principle applied to us. When we awoke, our minds were for a short while open and suggestible. The Devil chose that time to wage a whispering campaign to vex us with needless anxiety.

Once we had realised what was happening we found that we were able to resist his attacks. When we awoke, we commanded the 'whisperers' in the name of the Lord Jesus to go away. The effect was dramatic. We felt the demonic presence leave in a hurry. He tried a few more times, but we had uncloaked him and his mischief was spoilt. We had no more trouble.

Our confidence in the Lord was vindicated. One of the deacons in the Baptist church had said to us, with the Voice behind his words that we had come to recognise, 'God does not play games with us.' We had not come so far with him, believing in his guidance, so that he could mock us in disaster. The sale of the house went through in January 1991, just days before the bridging loan expired. We were heartily glad to be relieved of the burden.

Move to North Wales
Yet within days there was more uncertainty for us. The Chairman of Hydro announced at the Annual Dinner that the operation of which I was a member would be moved away from Havant to North Wales. I could see no alternative but to move with the Company and Marion agreed.

The process of setting up a new company and organising the move took longer than expected, but in March 1992 we felt it was time to put our lovely house in Chichester up for sale. It was our first house as newlyweds. We were sad to have to sell it so soon.

I was tempted to doubt the wisdom of my decision to

move from British Steel. It seemed that I had brought our new family into an uncertain predicament. Marion and I discussed it with each other and with one or two Christian friends who had witnessed all that had happened to us.

It is good occasionally to review events with the benefit of hindsight. Given our circumstances and the knowledge we had at the time of our marriage, we could not have done anything better than to move away from South Wales. Whatever may befall us, we would be wrong to view it as the Lord's discipline for our disobedience.

Despite the depressed state of the housing market, the house was sold with remarkable speed. It was exciting to see the process going so easily. We had a sense of the infinite power of our God to orchestrate events.

We began to look in North Wales for a suitable house. We would drive up to Chester on Friday nights, spend all Saturday looking at properties, try out a church on Sunday morning, then drive back to Chichester in the afternoon, a journey of nearly four hours. Despite many visits we were unsuccessful, both in settling upon a church and finding a house.

In mid-June 1992 we left Chichester with sadness. Our house was now occupied by its new owner and our furniture went into storage. We travelled up to North Wales and found a tiny furnished cottage to rent until we could decide upon where to live more permanently.

We were following our usual strategy—first find a good church, then look for a house. Ebenezer Baptist church in Mold had been recommended to us. We had visited it once or twice during our weekend house-hunting tours and had enjoyed the Sunday morning services. The pastor and the members of the congregation had made us very welcome. We began to feel that we had found our new spiritual home. Almost as soon as we had settled upon Ebenezer, we found the 'right' house within walking distance of the church. By September 1992 we had moved in and were reunited with our furniture.

We became quickly involved in the life of Ebenezer church. Because of our previous experience in youth work we were asked to join the leadership of the senior Covenanter group. In addition I have been asked occasionally to lead a Bible Study or Prayer Meeting.

Now, at the beginning of 1994, our life together seems to have reached a plateau. We are busy. Both of us have demanding jobs, Marion in the civilian staff supporting the police force and I as Health and Safety manager for Hydro. The Covenanter work and other church commitments occupy much of our spare time. Our parents are reaching the age when their increasing frailty requires us to visit them more often.

Our children are all grown up. The twins are 28 years old and teaching English in Hungary. Marion's older boy Philip, now 24, works for British Rail and is engaged to be married. Her younger boy David is still with us but plans to move to his own house. We will soon be alone together. It is normal to start married life as a couple and grow into a family. We started as a family and have now contracted to a couple.

In the closing lines of his gospel, John writes that all the world would not be big enough to contain the account of all that Jesus said and did. The Christian understands this statement. In each redeemed life there is a wealth of his words and deeds.

I have left out of this account many other personal experiences of the Lord's work in me. On the other hand I have attempted to write down those experiences which taught me something that I could share with the reader to God's everlasting praise and glory.

There is a stirring old verse by Rabbi ben Ezra via Robert Browning which might fittingly close my contribution.

> 'Grow old along with me!
> The best is yet to be;
> The last of life, for which the first was made;
> Our times are in his hand who saith,
> "A whole I planned! Youth shows but half.
> Trust God! See all, nor be afraid!" '

6

THE GOAL MORE IMPORTANT THAN THE ROUTE

Mary Mealyea

Some thirty years ago I sat enthralled as my primary six school teacher read our class the story of Gladys Aylward. I was not a Christian and in fact had never even been to Sunday School but God spoke to me through that book. My heart was captivated and I decided then that I wanted to be a missionary too. The seed was sown. Three years later, just before my fourteenth birthday, I came face to face with the God who had already begun to work in my life.

God deals with us all in a variety of ways. The apostle Paul's conversion and call were dramatic and sudden. For many, even today, God intervenes in their life in a dramatic fashion. It has not been so for me. God used a number of different strands to draw me to himself and to call me into full-time service, but mostly he has spoken through his still small voice.

My parents were not Christians when I was a child, but some of my relatives were. It was my grandmother who bought me my first Bible when I was eight or nine years old. She often spoke to me about God and taught me to pray to him. I don't remember hearing much about Jesus until the night I was converted. When I did hear about him it was like being introduced to someone I'd known for a long time but never before met. God had been quietly working in my young life for some time, preparing me for the night when I would discover how Jesus died for me. It was not hard to yield my life to the one who had already become a friend to me.

Desire to serve God grows
The seed of desire to be a missionary, already planted in my heart, very quickly grew once I became a Christian. I knew nothing about missionary life but I started to read books, given to me by kind Christian friends, about missionaries. I very soon became influenced by the lives of people like Isobel Kuhn, Jim Elliot and Hudson Taylor. What impressed me most was their unselfish desire to glorify God in their lives. Later, I read books by Amy Carmichael, James Packer, Martyn Lloyd Jones, some of the Puritans, and many others. I developed a love for reading and God used these books to influence the direction of my life. The natural longing to be a missionary was overtaken and became a settled belief that God was calling me to serve him. At that time it never occurred to me to think of doing anything else, but doubts came later.

My inward conviction that I should serve God overseas began to waver when I arrived at Dundee University and began to study medicine. I started thinking that life as a doctor in the West would be far more comfortable than life abroad. Of course I dressed it up in spiritual terms and I would argue with myself that I wasn't really sure if I was 'called'. I joined a missionary prayer group at University and went along to various missionary meetings in the Christian Union. It seemed to be expected of me and I couldn't think of a good enough reason not to go. After all I would pray for missionaries even if I myself would not be one.

I tried hard to remain objective, but despite the reluctance that seemed to have taken root I found myself drawn again to the missionary life. I remember being quite annoyed when I was asked to be missionary secretary on the committee for the Christian Union. Why couldn't they have asked me to do something else— anything apart from missionary secretary! I did not want to do it. I didn't want to get that involved. Eventually, I agreed, and as I recall events, I have to smile at the way in which God returned me to his objective for my life. I found my heart being captured again and by the end of the year I knew without a shadow of doubt that I would serve God overseas. I simply had to discover where.

In retrospect I was able to understand the significance of that struggle. Later, it would be important for me to be sure that my call to missionary work was not a mere childish desire but the will of God. I believe now that God used that time to make his will for my life clear and to test my willingness to obey.

Guidelines on guidance

Guidance can seem at times to be a delicate minefield which we have to navigate our lives through by varying degrees of skill. One wrong move and our plans blow up in our faces. We are faced with many choices and depending on which we make our lives will be fruitful and happy or frustrated and barren. We picture God wringing his hands and hoping we make the right choice. Or we view life as a game of Monopoly—land on the wrong square and we have to go back to the beginning or worse still, land in the bankruptcy courts or go straight to jail. I have experienced this kind of thinking and found that it leads to anxiety and fear. It bears absolutely no resemblance to the picture of guidance we are given in Scripture which reveals God not as passive spectator but rather as actively involved as the Guide of his people.

As a young Christian I learned an important lesson about guidance which has stayed with me and been a source of encouragement and comfort ever since. I was very much attracted to a young man who seemed equally attracted to me. We talked of marriage although no official engagement was made. I had prayed much about the relationship but nagging at the back of my mind were doubts. I knew I was too involved emotionally to break off the friendship—I wanted it too much. Yet there remained this unsettled feeling that there was something wrong. Perhaps this man was not God's choice of a partner for me. And so I prayed, 'Lord, if this relationship is wrong, then you break it up. I can't, but I do want your will in my life more than anything else, no matter what it costs and no matter how much it hurts.'

God heard and answered that prayer. When the relationship ended, I felt that my heart would break. But in the midst of the pain I knew that God loved me and had kept me safe. In the months that followed an important truth filtered down through my whole being and laid a foundational principle in my life. I had been about to make a mistake in my life; take a wrong turning. The man of my choosing was not God's choice. Because I truly wanted God's will in my life, therefore he would not allow me to make that mistake. It is my belief that when we sincerely seek God's will in our lives, whatever the cost, then we need have no fear of going in the wrong direction. I discovered that submission and obedience to the will of God would keep me safe.

Our lack of submission is invariably due to a failure to believe that God truly wants the best for us. It is when we fall for that particular temptation that we often make precipitate or harmful decisions. Hudson Taylor, the pioneer missionary to Inland China, writes of his own failure in the area of guidance when his initial proposal of marriage to the woman he was later to marry was turned down.

> We have need of patience and our faithful God brings us into experiences which, improved by his blessing, may cultivate us in this grace. Though we seemed to be tried at times almost beyond endurance, we never find him unable or unwilling to help and sustain us; and were our hearts entirely submissive to his will, desiring it and it only to be done, how much fewer and lighter would our afflictions seem to be. I have had much sorrow of late; but the principal cause I find to be want of willing submission to, and trustful repose in, God my strength. Oh to desire his will to be done with my whole heart and to seek his glory with a single eye.

I very quickly learned that God's will is not only the safest place to be but the best. Six months after that incident I met a young man who would later become my husband; but this time he was the man of God's choice.

A further six months on and God had healed my broken heart and I was ready to meet 'God's choice' again. We began a friendship which blossomed into love. God's choice was far superior to mine and we have had 20 years of happy marriage together.

Perhaps the two biggest decisions we make in life, apart from our decision to follow Jesus, are who we marry and what job or profession to go into. And in many ways the bigger of those two is whom we shall marry. It is easier to change our job than our marriage partner! Who we marry will shape the rest of our lives for good or ill and so it is vitally important to wait for God's choice. Harry has been an important influence for good in my life. He has always encouraged me to press on in my Christian life and to know Christ more fully. He has helped me to look at things rationally when I have been mixed up and confused. He has comforted and reassured. In short he has been and remains my best friend.

Many Christians are fearful, believing that God is hiding behind some celestial curtain waiting to see if we get 'our guidance' right or wrong. Others consider that he is a kill-joy who purposely leads us into difficult paths which he knows we will not enjoy. What perverse views of God these are! God is leading us every step of the way, hedging us around with his love, wanting the very best for us. What he asks of us is willing obedience. George McDonald has written, 'Obedience is the opener of the eyes', and it is here that we must start if we are serious about discovering more of what God is like and what he wants from our lives.

Harry's call to go overseas to work as a missionary had also started in childhood and grown into steady belief. When he chose to study architecture at university, it was with a view to using his professional qualification to gain entrance to a land which had closed the doors to missionary service. Therefore when Harry and I first met and began to be aware of a growing attraction, we were both independently anxious to find out how the other felt about work overseas. Indeed, on our first proper date our first conversation was about this very subject, such was the strength of call we both had. To our relief we discovered that we shared a desire for full-time service abroad. Should we have been surprised?

Marriage

For a variety of reasons, Harry and I were persuaded that we should get married the year before I finished my medical course. We wanted to be free to go abroad as soon as I finished my medical house jobs. By that time Harry would have finished at Bible College. We didn't want to get married just before my medical house jobs because we knew that that would be a tough year with the amount of 'on call' duty which would be required. It therefore seemed reasonable to get married just before my final year. I would already have done my written finals, the difficult part, leaving only the clinical exams to do.

Our wedding plans meant I would have to get permission from Dundee University, where I was studying, to transfer to the Glasgow Faculty. I would also have to get Glasgow University to accept me. We would also want my parents' blessing, which they gladly gave. Believing that God was in our plans we set the date of our wedding 'in faith.'

The final permission to transfer didn't come through until about two months before the date of our wedding. As we were both students we had little money and there were those who thought we should have waited to get married. I remember one dear friend asking out of concern, 'How will you manage, you can't live on fresh air.'

We were hoping to get a flat on the south side of Glasgow, but a few weeks before our wedding we were told that it was no longer available. What were we to do? We had nowhere to stay. Had we, as some had suggested, been too impatient? Throughout those days, God kept saying the same thing to us over and over again. He spoke in our daily reading of his word, he spoke through the preached word in church and he spoke through the encouragement of friends. The same word came to us again and again: 'your Heavenly Father knows that you need them', referring to the material needs of his children. It seemed in those days that wherever we went and whatever church service or Christian meeting we attended, the message was exactly the same, encouraging us to trust our heavenly Father to intervene. A week before our wedding, Harry received word to say that the flat we had wanted was now again available and at a rent which was unbelievably low.

As it turned out, the timing of our marriage was perfect. We discovered just before our wedding that my father had lung cancer. He died just three months after our wedding. Had we waited to get married, he would not have been there. A wedding without my father would have been very difficult for my mother to cope with. Had we not already made the decision to marry and go abroad before my father's death, it would have been difficult to do so after his death because of my mother's loss. Our Heavenly Father provided everything that we needed and that has been the pattern of our lives.

Call to Iran

Although we were both sure we were to work overseas, we were less certain where we would serve. Harry had for a number of years developed an interest in and burden for the Muslim people of the Middle East, but my interest had been more in the Far East. Harry was by this time at Bible College. One day he came home in great excitement. There had been a notice on the College notice board to say that there were opportunities for Bible teachers in Iran. There would be no need to rely upon professional qualifications to enter the country and therefore we could devote all our energy to church work. We began to find out more about Iran and about the missionary society [International Christian Fellowship, now a part of S.I.M. International] which had written to the Bible College. Harry became increasingly convinced that this was the right place for us to go to, but I was less sure. I think it was the Muslim culture which frightened me. Harry was persuaded that I should be as convinced as he was that this was the right move for us both.

Because of my previous broken relationship God left me in no doubt that Harry was the man I was to marry. Therefore I was able to reason that if God was calling Harry to Iran, as he obviously was, then he was also calling me there too. Many may see that as a rather simplistic approach but for me it was logical. Once I was willing to go, God gave me peace in my heart and the assurance that this was his will for us. Looking back now, I'm sure Satan was trying to thwart God's will and drive a wedge between husband and wife. Happily he didn't succeed and we both went to Iran with glad and willing hearts.

Life and the choices we make in it can seem so complicated and messy. Amy Carmichael has a very interesting illustration of God's dealings with us. She likens our life to a piece of tapestry. As we look at our lives we see the reverse side with the threads going all over the place, but God sees the picture on the right side. God is the Needleworker and our lives are the canvas. If we allow him, he will create a thing of beauty although that may not appear to be the case at the time. Indeed at times we may scratch our heads and wonder why everything seems so strange. God's ways are not our ways and events often do not work out as we expect. That has often been my experience.

When we went out to Iran we were prepared for a lifelong commitment. We could not have predicted that, within 18 months of arriving there, Iran would be plunged into a revolution that would eventually mean the end of our time in that country. We had spent two years in language study and now when we were about to enter what we thought would be our 'useful' phase, we had to leave. Imagine our bewilderment when, because of the revolution, we had to return home after only two years. This was a great disappointment and for a while a bitter blow. Before going out to Iran we had told our friends that it was the most stable country in the Middle East. The revolution was obviously no surprise to God. Surely he would not have sent us out there merely to learn the language and then bring us back again. What a waste? Had we made a mistake in going to Iran?

Could we discern any purpose in our recent past? When we first went to Iran, like most new missionaries we felt frustrated by our inability to communicate, to engage usefully in the work of mission. Both Harry and I had previously held responsible jobs. It was hard suddenly to feel so silly and unable to do anything. I had wrongly believed that our arrival in Iran signalled the end of our preparation for service and the beginning of our 'real' work. I was to learn that God is more interested in who we are than in what we do. The primary call of God is to Christlikeness; that is the real work. Whatever other work I was involved in was secondary to that.

As we look back we can see that God took us to Iran not so much to be of service to the church but to continue his work of grace in our hearts. We learned so much in Iran which has had a major influence on our lives. There is no waste in God's economy. No, Iran was not a mistake. A surprise to us but not to God. We were beginning to learn to trust God in the dark and to recognise that as we seek guidance from God for our lives, his major concern is to make us more like Jesus.

I have begun to look on my life as a series of steps, and at any stage God may choose to change the direction in which I am travelling. God is bold enough to take people halfway round the world in order to complete just one step in the plan he has for their lives. We can, at times unwittingly, attempt to limit God's work in our lives by believing that we travel in straight lines. We did this when we saw our call to work in Iran as a lifetime commitment. The service of some may well be to serve

God in a particular location all their lives. But on the other hand it may only be a stepping stone onto another path:

> 'In his heart a man plans his course,
> but the LORD determines his steps' (Proverbs 16:9)

Return to Scotland
Immediately upon our return we believed that our time at home could be part of further preparation for future service in Iran. Prior to our return Harry had been approached by the Iranian Presbyterian Church to work in Teheran. This work would have involved pastoring a church and teaching in a Bible School which they hoped soon to begin. It was suggested that, upon our return, Harry could upgrade his Dip. Th. from London University to a B.D. at a Scottish University. On completion of that study we hoped that the problems in Iran would be resolved, the situation stabilised and the way clear for our return to Iran.

Once we have asked God to guide clearly, the way forward may seem costly in the extreme. People often speak of the sacrifice of giving up things to serve God, but it has been my experience that God has given me far more than I have given him. Because we had planned to be in Iran for the rest of our working lives, we had taken all that we had with us in order to set up home there. After the revolution, when we were evacuated from Iran by the RAF, we were only allowed to bring out two suitcases. As we intended to return we had packed up what we could and stored it in the church in Tabriz, where we were living, to await our return.

So when we arrived home we had very little, and yet God so amazingly supplied all that we needed. There were places to stay—mostly rent free. One kind couple gave us the use of a car they didn't need. Glasgow University allowed Harry to do his B.D. in two years instead of three because of his having a Dip. Th. Because he was not doing his B.D. as a Church of Scotland candidate he had no grant, but we were able to get various awards and bursaries, and the Carnegie Trust paid all his fees.

At one point during our stay at home the need for further accommodation arose. The flat we were in was going to be required by someone else. I had what seemed like an unattainable desire to have a proper house with a garden. I even ventured to want a piano in the house. I remember telling a friend I was praying that God would give us such a house and he very gently chided me for having such grand desires. I should be content with much less. Of course I would have been content with whatever God provided, but God did give that house with a garden and a piano. And he continued to supply all our needs. God more than made up for all that we left behind in Iran.

What is God doing?

After two years, however, the door to Iran remained firmly closed. What would we do now? We still believed we were called to be missionaries. Although God had closed the way to Iran, we did not have any reason to believe that he was withdrawing our call to overseas service. But where should we be going now? Our mission approached us with the suggestion that we might consider service in Pakistan. This seemed quite a logical step. The language and script are in many ways similar to the Farsi which we had learned in Iran. The culture and religion would also be somewhat similar. There was the opportunity to engage in Bible teaching there with the Presbyterian Church.

After much prayer and discussion with Christian friends, whose counsel we valued, we were persuaded to proceed in this direction. We arrived in Pakistan and were devastated when I very quickly got ill and after only seven months had to return home to Glasgow. Medical opinion strongly advised against my return to Pakistan. At this stage Harry was obliged to pack up in Pakistan and come home. I was briefly thrown into a turmoil of self-doubt. Had we got our guidance wrong? Had we never been meant to be missionaries at all ? To our great pain some did suggest this to us.

This was a particularly sore time for me. I felt that it was my fault that we were 'failed missionaries'. I felt that I had let Harry down—how would he feel having to return from yet another mission field? I felt that I had let all our prayer partners down, and those who had supported us financially. Worst of all I felt that I had let God down. I was persuaded that I was a failure and that, along with physical weakness, left me bewildered and perplexed. What was God doing with us?

During that time of uncertainty God graciously drew near, comforting and encouraging me in the words of 1 Peter 5:10: 'And the God of all grace, who called you to his eternal glory in Christ, after you have suffered a little while, will himself restore you and make you strong, firm and steadfast.'

Samuel Rutherford's letters were also of tremendous encouragement to us at this time. The bulk of these were written when he had been forcibly removed from the pulpit and people whom he loved and was exiled to Aberdeen. In one letter he writes: 'When I am in the cellar of affliction I look for God's choicest wine.'

Rutherford's approach to suffering and disappointment was so positive. He expected it to furnish him with a rich harvest of blessing. We had not experienced Rutherford's intensity of sorrow and suffering, but we too discovered a God who draws near in the soreness of affliction with a richness of blessing which is hard to describe.

Those occasions when, humanly speaking, it appeared as though our plans were ending in disaster, have become God's seedbed for our spiritual growth and his furnace for tempering our spiritual metal. Despite the pain we experienced through the disintegration of our plans, we would not underestimate its value nor would we have sought to bypass it.

Iran and Pakistan were not mistakes but God's choice gifts to us. We learned lessons there which we will never forget. We were also privileged to meet some of God's choicest saints, people who have made our lives richer by their love and friendship and with whom we are still in touch.

Rethinking guidance
It appeared that the door to service overseas was closed to us and we were being steered back to Scotland yet again. This caused us to look at the whole business of guidance as we had never done before. In looking at

some of the teaching in the New Testament, we could see that Paul's goal in life was not so much to find out where God wanted him to be, but instead 'to know Christ and the power of his resurrection and the fellowship of sharing in his sufferings, becoming like him in his death, and so, somehow, to attain to the resurrection from the dead' (Philippians 3:10-11).

Paul had learned to be content whatever his circumstances or location because Christ himself was the great Circumstance and Location of his life.

We discovered that books on guidance are a comparatively modern phenomenon and, for example, one would be hard pressed to find the subject dealt with by any of the Puritan divines. And when we ask why that should be so, we discover that their great emphasis was not where they were but how they lived. They made holiness of life and obedience to God's word their aim. With those objectives as their priority other matters fell into place.

We read again of Paul's setbacks and geographical redirection. Acts 16 describes the strange path along which he was led into Macedonia. Paul began to head towards the province of Asia, but the Spirit, exactly how we are not told, prevented him from preaching there. He then attempted to go to Bithynia but again the Spirit prevented him. Again we do not know what means of restraint were used but the important thing is that Paul headed off in two directions which he had obviously thought were right and found that he had been wrong. I am quite sure that Paul did not sit down in despair, wring his hands and say, 'Woe is me. I must have been mistaken in my guidance.' He was called to preach God's word and so he simply moved on to the next place. Paul then had his vision of the Macedonian man asking for help, and he immediately assumed that this was the direction in which he should go.

It has been my experience that often I may start off heading for place or work A and end up in place or work B. But that does not mean it was wrong to head off for place A in the first place. C. G. Moore puts it well when he says:

It is by no means enough to set out cheerfully with your God on any venture of faith. Tear into small-est pieces any itinerary for the journey your im-agination may have drawn up. Nothing will fall out as you expect. Your guide will keep to no beaten road ... He knows no fear and he expects you to fear nothing whilst he is with you. The clinging hand of his child makes a desperate situation a delight to him. A true walk with God will do more to awaken awe, wonder and amaze-ment in your soul than would a century of travel through the sights of earth ... to take you to his 'end' by the way you know would profit you little. He chooses for you a way you know not, that you may be compelled into a thousand communica-tions with himself which will make the journey forever memorable to him and to you.

It became increasingly clear as we thought through these issues, talked them over with friends and used the minds which God has given us, that he now wanted us to exercise our ministry in Scotland. Harry applied to and was accepted by the Church of Scotland as a minister.

This approach to guidance is markedly different from that which I employed as a new convert. Then I used to try to discover God's will by randomly opening my Bible and reading the first verse my eyes fell upon. I soon discovered the folly of this approach. I was looking for an easy and quick answer. There was no work on my part, no exercise of faith, no persevering prayer. I remember being in a friend's home and after dinner 'the promise box' was passed around, like a box of after-dinner mints. Everyone drew out a promise and took this as God's special word to them. If we build our lives on this approach to Scripture then we are building a very shaky edifice which one day will surely come crumbling down around us. James Packer, commenting on the subject of guidance, writes: 'In our quest for guidance we become our own worst enemies and our mistakes attest to our nuttiness in this area.'

When one thinks of the different methods Christians use, we are obliged to agree with Packer. Christians often depend on their feelings, circumstances and fleeces, while others rely on a whole variety of Biblical contortions which often prove to be Biblical distortions including opening the Bible and reading the first verse the eyes fall on. How nutty can we get?

God expects us to be mature in our choices
As I have grown in the Christian life, I have realised the need to build Biblical principles into my life. I have done this through personal Bible study and by sitting under the ministry of God's word in church. This has led to a discovery of God's character and will. I have begun to learn, albeit slowly, how to put these principles into

practice in different situations. Past lessons are applied to new situations. In this way, when presented with a choice, the former fearful anxiety has been replaced with a quiet confidence concerning God's will in a whole range of issues. God has given us an intelligence which includes reason and logic and he expects us to employ it. As we mature as Christians, God expects more of us. When we are babes in Christ he spoon-feeds us, but as we grow he expects us to feed ourselves from all the rich resources he has given us.

My youngest daughter, who is just three, is quite independent and often wants to choose her own clothes for the day. She will go to her room and return with a very odd selection of clothes. She would quite happily wear trousers and a blouse with a dress on top. And of course none of the colours match. She is not yet old enough to choose wisely for herself. She needs help and guidance. My oldest son of twelve however would be quite indignant if I laid out his clothes for the morning. He is old enough to choose for himself. Likewise, when we are young Christians, we need help in a whole number of areas of our lives and God graciously leads in these areas. But as we grow in our knowledge of God and his will there are many decisions which God expects us to make for ourselves.

I remember hearing of a couple who would pray for guidance before they did anything. What clothes to put on in the morning , what to have for breakfast, every detail of their lives became a matter for direct guidance. My first reaction was—how spiritual! Yet as I thought about it, I realised that they were living in a spiritual straitjacket. We are not robots. If you are deeply concerned about whether you should wear blue or red socks and think it necessary to pray about it and search for a Biblical theology of colours, your life must be absolutely miserable. God does not intend us to be frozen in anxiety each time we have a choice to make. God has given us standards and principles to regulate our behaviour and when these are not violated he has given us freedom to make a great many decisions in life. Some people can tiptoe nervously through life or wobble fearfully on their acrobatic tightrope. They live in craven fear of God and of missing an invisible path laid out for them. The fact that God has a plan for our lives should not strike terror in our hearts, but rather promote joyous assurance.

There will be times when guidance is far from clear. On these occasions light is often shed as we quietly continue with what we know to be our duty. As a doctor, I have discovered that sometimes the diagnosis of an ill patient is not immediately clear, and sometimes one has to wait to see how the illness develops and then a clearer idea of the diagnosis is possible. It's as if you have to wait for a few more pieces of the jigsaw to fit before you can begin to see the full picture. Guidance for me has sometimes been like that. I have had to wait and see how things develop and in the meantime carry on with what I already know God wants me to do.

I think we often make guidance more complicated than we need and I know that there have been times when I have got myself into quite a state of anxiety over making some decision or other. This has usually been, in my case, overwork. Which job to apply for or accept? I can remember often praying, 'Lord, if you would just tell

me what you want me to do, I will do it whatever it is.'
Anxiety is often rooted in our fear of making a decision
which might complicate our lives and the fruitfulness of
our service.

At such times I have had to remind myself of two
things. First, if I sincerely want God's will he will not let
me make some terrible mistake. Secondly, God is more
interested in me as a person than in what I do. The
decision about what job to take or what house to live in
is overshadowed by a more important consideration;
how can I be made more like Jesus and my life better
reflect that likeness? In other words it might not be a life
or death issue as to whether I take a job in dermatology
or cardiology. The important thing is, that whatever the
decision, I am able to live to the praise of his glory in this
new situation.

Fear paralyses us and God is not a God of fear. We are
not meant to fear guidance but rather rest in the sure
knowledge that our Heavenly Father is gently leading
us. When God has been leading me to a change of
direction he has always done so gently. There is a sweet
reasonableness associated with the drawing work of
God's Holy Spirit. If I have felt I was being bulldozed or
encouraged to bypass my God-given thinking proc-
esses, I have usually found that this pushing has come
from the enemy.

In my experience God's leading has become clearer
as my mind has been engaged and been persuaded of the
reasonableness and logic behind the decision. This is
what has been described as 'sanctified common sense'.
This requires a mind which is conditioned by Scripture,
not by a specific verse but by broad Biblical principles.

This is the renewed mind which Paul advocates in Romans 12:2, the mind/attitude of Christ which Paul encourages the Philippians to adopt in Philippians 2:5. Paul, writing to the Ephesians, again emphasises the need to use our minds, 'Do not be foolish but understand what the Lord's will is' (5:17).

Scottish Director of CARE
During our time abroad and at home I had come across a number of folk who were depressed and not coping with life, others who had various kinds of mental illness. I therefore became interested in the area of psychiatry. When we moved to Paisley, where Harry had his first charge, the opportunity arose to work in a hospital conveniently close to where we were living and so I accepted.

After I had been working in psychiatry for a few years I became involved with the work of CARE (Christian Action, Research and Education). I found what they were doing very interesting and when I was asked to be the Scottish Director I was ready to accept. The offer came at a time when I was thinking of a change from psychiatry. Because of the nature of the work I would be able to work from home and fit in times around our family needs. There were other factors and circumstances which confirmed to me that this move was from God.

Likewise when I decided to leave the decision was an obvious one. CARE had grown in Scotland. The work that I had taken on had expanded. There were increasing invitations to speak all over Scotland and with my family commitments I could not accept them all. It was a time when I felt strongly that my children needed me to be home more. When I had started in the job I worked from home, but soon the need had arisen to have an office. So I had to make a decision. If CARE was to continue to grow I would have to travel more and be away from home. But I felt I could not do that because of the family. It was obvious to me therefore that my time with CARE had come to an end. They needed someone who could commit more time not less, and so I resigned as soon as a replacement could be found. I believe that family responsibilities are an important factor which can shape our thinking concerning the kind of service in which we are engaged.

Latterly my guidance for what I should be doing has been strongly influenced by my family circumstances. I now have four children and being a mother is a full-time commitment, as is my role as a minister's wife. I am not able to take on the same number of speaking engage- ments. There are certain times of the day when I am committed to being available for the children, therefore I am not free for other things. Is staying at home to do the ironing and help the children with their homework less spiritual than going out to a large Christian gathering to give an address? Surely not, if the ironing is what God has given me to do.

The goal of God's guidance—Christlikeness
In the past I have been overly concerned about where I should be and what I should be doing. Now I can see that the geography of where I am and the particular work I am doing may be important; but far more important is the fact that wherever I am and whatever I am doing I do it

to God's glory, and that day by day I am allowing God, through whatever means, to change me and make me more like Jesus. We can think that if we make a wrong choice we may miss the boat of Christian service altogether. We forget that Jesus is the pilot of the boat and when he invites us on board he is not going to leave without us. There is no need to allow fear to paralyse us nor do we need to rush around in a blind panic.

There have been times when I am sure that I have made mistakes, usually because I have allowed myself to be rushed into a decision. On other occasions I have made my own plans and then convinced myself that these were really God's will. Sometimes God allows us to live with our mistakes but that does not mean we are irretrievably out of his will. He is a God of new beginnings and he is also an amazing salvage expert. I am convinced that where our hearts and wills truly desire to follow Jesus he will not allow us to stray far or for long and certainly not in a manner which would be harmful.

The goal is more important than the route travelled. That goal is clear. It is to make us more like Jesus. When we grasp that, or better when that thought grasps us, then in all our decision-making we will want to ask God for whatever will make us more like Jesus. We will often be taken along strange routes. They make no sense to us. They leave us baffled and puzzled. We may feel that God is wasting our time and potential for service. We need to stand back from the picture and see the goal of God's guidance, which is Christlikeness. We will learn to thank God for the darkest valleys and sorest furnaces, because like Job we will surely come out refined by being tried in the fire.

THE GOAL MORE IMPORTANT THAN THE ROUTE

When we ask for guidance our motive shouldn't be our pleasure but rather God's glory. When we do so we will find guidance a far broader thing than we had previously conceived. It was this kind of thinking which prompted Augustine to say, 'Love God with all your heart and do what you like'. Understood correctly that is not a recipe for sin but for enjoying Christian liberty. Probably the most important lesson I have learned in my life is that the where and why and what are not so important. It is our closeness to Jesus. And when we walk close to him, with our eyes on him, then the where and why and what will fall into place.

7

BETTER WITH HINDSIGHT

Joel Edwards

Deep roots—small branches
On a clear, crisp day in May 1960 a British Overseas
Airways Corporation plane from Kingston, Jamaica,
touched down on the Heathrow tarmac. It rolled adjacent
to the distinctive Queen's building and came to a gentle
stop. A plane load of trans-Atlantic travellers stepped
out into the fraudulent sunshine to face the unknown in
Great Britain.

At eight years old, I was a fellow-pilgrim on this
flight which seemed to last for days. Together with my
two older sisters I filed apprehensively to the waiting
building to endure the mysterious process of being
welcomed to our 'Mother Country', before emerging
into the waiting arms of our mother and other relatives.
The final leg of the expedition—a thirty mile-journey
into a postwar London which still bore the scars of war—
seemed to pass in a moment of unconsciousness before
we finally arrived at an address which could only, it
seemed to me, have been an industrial complex; the
terraced properties stretched interminably towards the
horizon with monotonous similarity. When the front
door closed behind us with a possessive thud, the reality
of the situation came home to me—I was in England.

With hindsight, that moment of bewildering and

intense culture shock was like stepping into the vestibule of God's purpose with a rucksack of formative experiences on my back. The day which had begun over twenty-four hours earlier was precipitated by the sudden disappearance of our mother, who had fled the domestic tensions of our home in Kingston and emigrated to England some two years earlier. Even at the tender age of six, my memories of home were a curious combination of childhood pleasures and the horror of waking early to the cries of an abused mother. Fatherhood was a concept rather than an experience, and even now positive recollections of a father-son relationship during those early years are few and far between.

But at the heart of my embroidered childhood recollections —school days and passing friendships—were the deep impressions of Elder Shaw and the Newtown Church in Kingston. Elder Shaw was a respected and revered, charismatic and inspirational preacher. He preached with a passion which not only kept me awake, but which also convinced me that he believed what he preached. At that age his words were unimportant to me, but his enthusiasm was infectious. When my mother reminded me in later years that I often posed as a miniature Shaw lookalike, it made immediate sense to me. Her account was entirely consistent with my own imprecise memories of stalking through the Rastafarian colony of Trenchtown, with an air of anticipation, to worship at Newtown and hear Elder Shaw preach. It seems I was not alone because the building was always filled with people caught up in responsive worship to the preaching of the word.

Similarly, vague memories of a major evangelistic

mission persist. It may have been a Billy Graham or T. L. Osborne visit to Kingston during the 1950's, but I have always cherished the memory of being taken in the twilight to witness the impact of the gospel on a mass open-air audience. No words accompany the recollection, no themes or faces, only the notion of the spoken word piercing the night air and eliciting a response from those present.

I was one born out of due time. Actually I was not supposed to happen, and so my arrival in October 1951— shortly after a major hurricane—was totally unexpected. When I arrived on the scene, my mother, aged forty-five, had already had five children and experienced a number of still-births. She delights to tell the story of my impending birth and to this day it remains one of her favourite party pieces! Shortly before my birth she dreamt I would be a boy and was directed to name me Joel.

Having lived with this story for many years I have to admit it has always provided me with a combination of comfort and consternation. In dark periods it has been a silent pilot light of encouragement, such a deeply personal part of my own consciousness that I have seldom mentioned it and never committed it to writing before this point. However, it has helped me understand God's willingness sometimes to identify his purpose for us from a very early stage.

Of course, this kind of landmark gives no guarantee of a carefree existence, nor does it provide unobstructed light for every subsequent step in life. So often it is rather the recollection of what God has said, or the quiet confidence that we, or others on our behalf, may have heard God speak and a willingness to keep going when the silent times come, as surely they do.

In retrospect, these were the earliest memories of a germinating ministry. Admittedly, the roots went very deep even though the branches were still so small.

What's a coloured person?

Over the years I have tried to recapture my first day in an English school, but without success. My earliest memories of primary school are cumulative rather than specific, a very painfully acute awareness of being different and that my difference made me an oddity. I still recall my accent launching other students into fits of laughter. I attracted attention simply by being myself. The patronising compliments and underhanded jokes about my hair and complexion made me, to some extent, the centre of attention in the classroom. That seemed to be a high price to pay for what felt like the pillaging of my personhood.

In Jamaica, I was just a boy. In England I became a 'coloured person'. How strange! So genuine was the depth of my confusion that I was totally convinced that coloured televisions were special issues for 'coloured folk'! This matter of being different was never discussed or dealt with in any meaningful way. It was the fabric of one's existence as a black person in those pre-Black Consciousness days, but a whole generation of black and immigrant people were given no tools of awareness with which to preserve themselves. As always, the young were the most susceptible. The eroding impact of 'differentness' was silently unrelenting. Never explained, it never made sense. One just felt the pervasive mantle of cultural confusion cloaking self-respect as a great bird of prey smothers its victim.

It was only with the hindsight of some twenty years that I was able to see how deep my confusion became. It was particularly invidious because it went unnoticed. Like the small seed of a wild bush falling carelessly into the ground, so ideas of inadequacy wedged themselves in my growing self-awareness.

It was never said out loud, but I became convinced that to be different was probably the same as being daft. Normality meant being abnormal and developing two distinct lifestyles which never met in conscious dialogue. The truly Caribbean boy stayed at home and in church within the security of all that was familiar and affirming. The 'coloured' boy ventured out to school, always on the lookout to assimilate acceptable behaviour which would allow him the luxury of social and cultural conformity. It was hard to be critical of a world I did not fully understand. And so the fact that I only ever entered the home of my other 'coloured' friend, Errol Rowe, and never even passed the front door of my white friend, Martin Hollingsworth, was always an unquestioned mystery.

But it wasn't all bad news in those early years. The silent traumas of my new lifestyle in northwest London were not all depressing—even though it was difficult. Undoubtedly, we were amongst the poor in London, but we didn't necessarily think of ourselves in those terms—even when we lived four in a bedroom or picked up our vouchers for free school meals. Not even my near miss when the chimney from our three-storey home came tumbling about my feet registered for me our relative poverty. God was already at work upon me in my painful transition between cultures and the coming demands of teenage years.

Apart from my home environment, the greatest stabilizing influence was a steady awareness of God, fostered and sustained by my constant exposure to the worship environment of a small group of black Christians, a bus ride and train journey away in Kilburn. There, in that self-contained environment, I had a distinct sense of unidentified security. No extra effort to *be* was necessary. No-one tried to stroke your hair or laughed when you spoke. Something else was reassuring: people seemed to believe what they said and, like Newtown Church in Kingston, the preachers kept me awake.

The last one's a monkey

I can never quite remember how old I was when I became a Christian. It's always one of those tantalising questions which sets my mind in motion on a precision-hunt in the same way that one attempts to recall the exact details of an old movie in order to finish the crossword puzzle.

I may have been ten or eleven. I know I was still in primary school and that the event took place during a convention in Handsworth, Birmingham. A pre-motorway trip from London to Birmingham in 1962 was like a major expedition which started before sunrise and felt longer than the five-day event itself. If you could survive the usual hazards of adult rectitude, conventions were fun.

I met up with a new friend called 'Bunnie'. I imagine 'Bunnie' was a nickname he acquired for his bright dancing eyes, his mischievous grin and furtiveness; it seemed an excellent association of ideas. We became inseparable until the time we sat together at the front row of the meeting and listened with amusement to the altar invitation. 'The last one to the altar is a monkey,' said Bunnie. There was to be a count of three before the race to the altar began. I did not want to be a monkey and so set off in great haste at the count of three. On arriving at the altar rail I looked to either side and then over my shoulder where I saw Bunnie doubled in hysterical laughter. Disappointed and cheated I felt there was nothing for it but to assume the position and appear to pray. I would settle things with Bunnie later and, in any event, it would be unwise to leave the altar as my mother would probably be watching.

I cannot describe clearly what happened next. What I do remember though is that I was overwhelmed by a terrible sense of sin and simultaneously by an even greater degree of forgiveness. I have no idea how hard or how long I cried. It seemed that my awful awareness of sin was compensated for by a special facility of repentance and a limitless supply of grace. When I stood I felt freer than was possible to describe and cleaner than I have ever known. I never saw Bunnie again.

It is always difficult for me to recount that momentous event—the greatest event in my life—without including the Bunnie factor. Somehow the event is inconceivable without him. Nothing else in my pre-teenage conversion provided me with a rationale for responding to an appeal after an irrelevant sermon than my fleeting friendship with him—somebody I would not now recognise if he stood beside me on an underground platform, or even served me for many years from the other side of a bank counter. But undoubtedly God used Bunnie to change my life.

Faith, failure and faithfulness

It was not long before secondary school came along. I was at school for many years but I did not understand what it was all about. My education at Sir William Collins Secondary School, near Camden Town in London, represented a significant block of life-experience between the ages of eleven and nineteen. It never occurred to me to consider doing my 'A' levels at Sixth Form College and so I remained in my third sixth year (one of only three such specimens of endurance) and had to run the gauntlet of jokes about becoming a grandfather while still being at school!

The madness of teenage years during this period was a bitter-sweet experience. It was that perfect recipe for the development which came with problems and privileges. Many of my negative perceptions about myself persisted, amongst them the now growing recognition of what it meant to be poor. The final ignominy was to stand in the free-dinner line well into sixth form and to suffer the silent shame of collecting the grant for the free school uniforms from the 'special shop' in Tottenham Court Road. The desire to have and to be wanted ran deeper than I had realized in my first year of school.

Sir William Collins was an average-to-above-average London comprehensive with its usual concoction of bullies, truants, overstretched staff and a well-meaning headmaster attempting to keep things together. It became evident that there was at least one way to make money and a name for myself: stealing—my principles and character did not lend themselves to extortion. Woolworths, and shops with accessible stationery materials, developed a particular attraction for me. It was an ideal business: steal from the rich and sell to the poor, who would usually be first, second or third year pupils. It was strange how acceptable this behaviour became in the twilight morality of the school playground—which had absolutely no relationship to my church or home life. The school experience, held in a watertight compartment of secular morality, rapidly distanced me from the co-existing spirituality which belonged to the church.

The inevitable came one day while I was 'shopping' in Woolworths and a low key, high impact arrest was made. I still have vivid memories of being locked in an unfriendly cell where I began thinking more clearly than I had done for many months. In the darkness of my cell, I began to see clearly how easy it was to betray God as so many of the Sunday School characters had done. In that stillness I was shocked into what was really a deeper conversion. I had to learn as an eleven-year-old Christian that it was necessary for my behaviour and my experience of God to meet each day.

In a strange way the sudden conclusion of my illegal trading brought me a new lease of life. It was as though the security guard was not the only one to catch up with me. The realization of my own frail vulnerability was a great and cleansing awakening. The awful awareness that I had let God down was matched by the consciousness that God was unwilling to abandon me to my own abject failure. Forgiveness and renewal came to me like rays of sunshine on a cloudy day. In fact I acquired a new attitude to school life which, on reflection, became more consistent with a worship lifestyle and narrowed the gap between church and school. I learned for the duration of my school days that in many ways it was easier to be consistent than to be a chameleon!

Not all my friends understood my faith and in my naivety I failed to realise that what I thought was light-hearted humour about my faith was actually schoolboy ridicule. But not everyone was like that. For a significant number of fellow-pupils and staff the predictability of a lifestyle which was transparently religious in the playground, as well as the classroom, commanded a level of respect which stood me in good stead for the remainder of my school days. I became the first black House Captain, and eventually left school having had the responsibility of Captain for two years.

During those formative years of my Christian development God was active, quietly putting down the foundations on which my future work would be built. The single-minded commitment of a teenage boy travelling ten miles to church two or three times each week must have appeared as something of a strange phenomenon to anyone who cared to notice it. My insatiable appetite for God drove me to seek him out in any gathering I suspected he would attend. Small prayer gatherings and Bible studies, large conventions or house meetings were all the same to me. My attendance was motivated neither by the venue nor by personalities. I was determined only to get close to God and to seek every opportunity to do so.

So consumed was I by my passion for God that for all those years I failed to notice how unusual my behaviour was. I only noticed that other teenagers seldom showed up at the same places! But my concern was not to compare my devotion to God with other people, it was simply that during this time being in God's presence gave meaning to my life.

It took many years to realise that God was teaching me to be faithful. That willingness to be anonymously passionate about God was far more important a discipline than my teenage years could rationalise. I learned that being with God was even more important than doing things for God. Faithfulness is nurtured in solitude and not in the spotlight of publicity. Eventually, faithfulness brings its own rewards.

Stepping out

My first mini-sermon was delivered in my home church when I was nineteen. Although I had shared my testimony on many occasions prior to that time, this short address was a very memorable occasion for me. In fact it was the culmination of a whole series of preparatory steps.

My first invitation to speak publicly came shortly after my dramatic conversion. Our then Youth Leader, Ron Brown, attempted to persuade me to testify in our local church shortly afterwards. He was gentle and persuasive; I was small and very frightened. I declined the offer! But Sunday School days and the range of youth activities gave me an excellent head start.

Our second Youth Leader, Miss McKenzie (to whom I owe a great deal) was a very demanding woman who approached her task with the rigour of a sergeant major! We frequently disagreed and in our early teens resented the activities which seemed to be an unreasonable intrusion on our precious time. But Sister McKenzie was persistent. The group songs and recitations, choir practices and Sunday School sessions gave us an ability to stand in a packed hall with some poise and confidence. In those early years I was helped to take my first steps by a woman with whom I seldom related well, and whose own die-hard commitment I did not appreciate or understand.

I developed a love for the guitar in my late teens and frequently played both in the worship situation and as a member of an amateur Gospel group until my late twenties. After Sister McKenzie, the guitar taught me to step forward and brought me into the centre of things in the local church. It gained me respect amongst the adults. But it did nothing for my spiritual hunger. The two things came together one very strange Sunday evening when I was seventeen.

Along with a number of other youngsters we were rehearsing before the evening service when I was asked to leave the group in order to spend time welcoming a visitor who had stationed herself nervously towards the back of the church building. I swallowed my resentment and set off on my mission, noticing that this visitor was an older English woman. We introduced ourselves and she proceeded to bombard me with a list of questions about myself. Then she asked the question I feared most, 'Have you been baptised in the Holy Spirit?' It was not a theological question. In my own heart it was a profoundly experiential one, for this was the thing I most desired from God above all other things. 'Not yet,' was my standard response to the question, 'I'm still waiting on the Lord.' That usually deflected attention on to other matters, but to my amazement this frail and ashen woman refused to let it drop.

It was at that point that she told me that in the normal scheme of things she would be in her own church, but God had woken her from a mid-afternoon nap and sent her to this church which she had not known before. Her punch-line was very memorable. 'I believe God has sent me to see you,' she said, 'and to tell you that he will use you if you remain humble before him, but if not, you will forfeit the blessing.' I thanked her and asked to be excused. I cannot clearly remember the remainder of the evening. I do recall thinking that the word 'forfeit' sounded very quaint outside the song book and that it occurred to me that God must have been paying attention to my intense hunger. We prayed the opening prayer for the evening and when I opened my eyes she was gone.

I was nineteen when I received the baptism of the Holy Spirit. That day I was, in the words of C. S. Lewis, 'surprised by joy'! It happened during a period of unparalleled frustration and impatience. I felt my hunger for God had become so intolerable that I would die. My prayers in that period were no more than staccato utterances which punctuated my deep dissatisfaction. My last prayer the day before was particularly brief. Walking under a bright blue sky I had prayed, 'Lord, if you don't help me, I have had it!' I had forgotten my prayer the next day as I stood in church observing others worship. It was then that a surge of joy swept over me such as I had never experienced before and a nearness of God's presence came which accentuated my worship to a degree I had never known previously. Great torrents of praise poured out from me, carried along by a language

I did not recognise. In that moment I understood, as never before, that perfect love drives out fear.

When I stood to give my first mini-sermon some weeks later, I was not prepared for the outflow which overtook me. My theme was the Second Coming. If I had that same sermon to preach today I would wish to review many points in the content, but I will always cherish that sense of God's presence which accompanied me in the pulpit. It is possibly what the Pentecostal preachers and Dr Martyn Lloyd-Jones frequently referred to as the 'unction' of God. When I sat down again it occurred to me that I had not forfeited the blessing. I felt as though, after years of quiet preparation, I was stepping forward.

A new sense of direction

I have never understood the assumption that a particular experience of God's blessing automatically leads to an undervaluing of the word. Following this turning-point experience of blessing, my next quest was to study the Bible. A year earlier my plans to do a university degree in Sociology collapsed and although I was not an academic student, my desire to go on to further studies did not desert me with my disappointing grades. My local pastor, Rudolf Kennedy (who was also my mentor and friend), told me about a new degree in theology at a Bible College north of London, and wondered if I might be interested in following it through. Within weeks I found myself being interviewed for a place at London Bible College. I just made it before the drawbridge was raised on the application waiting list.

London Bible College was a culture shock. More accurately it was a series of shocks. In common with many other students I was called upon to deal with the transition of leaving home for the first time. The greater shock was to realise just how insular my church experience had been. The academic, interdenominational and international world of Bible College in 1972 was a stark contrast to the intimate environment of the Black Pentecostal Church. I had a feeling of being thrust out unceremoniously from the womb of my former church experience to the glaring lights of a large, confusing world. I met the word *evangelical* for the first time, and was obliged to catch up with the significance of household names I had never encountered. My experience of church life went from the free spontaneity of syncopated worship to a more cerebral devotional response, and my hitherto monochrome understanding of God in the world was shaken into a kaleidoscope of evangelical perspectives. Gradually it became apparent to me that others outside of my own tradition could *possibly* get to heaven after all, and that women wearing cosmetics and jewellery could conceivably be Christians!

Perhaps my greatest shock was to realise that I really wasn't English. No one ever told me otherwise but I had always felt that it had been a prerequisite for success. Here at London Bible College, for the first time in my life, I knew what it was to live twenty-four hours every day with two bona fide English gentlemen in Aldis House, across the corridor from Dr H. D. McDonald's private flat.

By being exposed to a multiplicity of cultures I began, for the first time, to discover myself again. This new-found discovery led me to take a few tentative steps further in self-discovery. I began to realise how little I knew about myself. This lesson in self-awareness gained new momentum by an incident which happened during my second year. I was very close to three fellow-students, two Scottish and one white American (our partnership exploits included a midnight raid on a rival Bible College during our final year!). In the process of building up a modest library, I acquired my first two books on black history which were spotted by one of my colleagues during a brief pre-table-tennis visit to my room. He reached over to my bookshelf, extracting these two works from the others with a startling question. 'Will the *real* Joel Edwards step forward?' he requested. We were, and remain, good friends. He meant no harm by it but its impact on my awareness of myself was incalculable.

Now I knew for sure that I was a black person who belonged to Britain. I was not an Englishman.

I learnt a great deal during my three years at LBC and I regard them as one of the most constructive and God-given opportunities in my life. I went into student life with no preconceptions about future ministerings or opportunities. As I told my local church at my temporary farewell, I went with 'no strings attached' and no other ambition than to study God's word. Unknown to me, amongst the mysteries of the Greek conjugations and the complexities of theology, God was simply working out his own quiet purpose for my life. In all the ups and downs of those three magnificent and precious years, I learned things I had never contemplated, met people whose world mingled briefly with mine, and I discovered that God was much bigger than I had been led to believe. Apparently, he fathered non-Pentecostals too! Most of all I learned about myself. Saying goodbye to LBC was very difficult. I felt instinctively that it had been a springboard in my life, but I had no idea where I was likely to land.

On Probation

In all my years I have only been unemployed for three months. It was unbearable. My intention was to head for the Probation Service and fulfil a private goal I had cherished in the latter part of my sixth form. My application to the Middlesex Probation Service for the post of an ancillary worker took longer than I had anticipated. The three months dragged by interminably until the interview opportunity finally came.

The interview in the Tottenham office, overlooking the Court, seemed more a game of wits than an interview. For me, it was an opportunity to find out whether this really was the right direction to go in, and it was evident that my interviewers were totally bemused by an applicant with a recently acquired degree in theology. 'I wouldn't have thought that a degree in theology was very relevant for work as an ancillary worker,' said the main interviewer. 'I would have thought so,' came my off-the-cuff response. 'The Bible is, after all, very concerned about people and I can think of no better preparation for dealing with human relationships than a study of the Bible.' Evidently it worked.

Eighteen months as an ancillary worker seemed a long sentence, but it provided an excellent and well-used path to social work training at Middlesex Polytechnic, and eventual employment with the Inner London Probation and After-Care Service in 1978. Those twelve years of 'service' gave me my first opportunity to see the real world and to understand, as never before, the impact of our sinful nature on our community. Admittedly, one only saw the 'problem people' who had made their way, whether justly or unjustly, through the penal system. I learned about my own humanity through that experience, and frequently realised that my own background—black youth, single parent, poor—made me a typical candidate for criminality. So close was my social affinity to many of my clients in North London that I sometimes felt I counselled myself through their situations. Ostensibly, those twelve years were my Sinai experience before my burning bush.

Looking back, I see I was being trained in different ways simultaneously and yet was totally unaware of it. My return to my home church from full-time study was a difficult transition. There was no doubt about it: I had changed and few people were able to appreciate my new world-view. Wider lenses had been fitted to my vision of the Church, and the insularity of my own experience as a black Pentecostal was now being changed. For three years I had seen a wider horizon and paddled out in an attempt to meet it. My love and appreciation of all the people had not diminished and my commitment to my local church remained unabated, and was now fuelled by a new desire to serve and to pour out all I had obtained. But I had to realise that to do so would be unkind and unhelpful. My pilgrimage need not be everyone's journey. Now I needed to understand the importance of having something to offer and yet reserving it for the appropriate time.

A year later I was appointed as the local Youth Leader. Incidentally, this was the obvious route to promotion for a Bible College graduate in my kind of church: Youth Leader, local Pastor and finally an Area-Supervising Pastor. My stint as Youth Leader lasted for little over a year. Locally, my whole ministry was a series of unending frustrations. I did not see eye to eye with my local leadership and was totally linked with the rise and fall of the spiritual tide of the youth work.

For years my sole responsibility in the local church was to play the organ on a Sunday. There were times when frustration drove me to distraction and I was convinced that there was little sense in all that was happening around me. It was in this period, however, that I unwittingly learned the power of patience. To sit passively each week with a heart pounding to serve, whilst absorbing misunderstanding and mistrust, was very difficult and made no sense at the time. But I simply knew that God wanted me there to *love*; I seldom stepped on the platform during those difficult years, but quietly God gave me a ministry of encouragement to others simply by allowing me to *be* there.

I didn't notice the irony of my situation until years after. In 1978 I began teaching at our denominational evening Bible classes—the Ebenezer Bible Institute (EBI). A year later I was appointed as the co-ordinator of the programme with full responsibilities for a hundred evening students and eight staff, including my own minister! What was truly amazing was that this responsibility was given to me although I was not a licensed minister within the church. It was a gesture of trust which I appreciated. My work with the Ebenezer Bible Institute lasted for five years and taught me the importance of teaching ministry in the local church.

My ability to cope during this difficult period of

development was helped by my recent marriage. Carol and I had known each other for five years before we were married in 1976. In fact she had accompanied me on my initial trip to London Bible College. Our courtship—very lengthy by 1970's standards—was a rather difficult one at times, filled with significant periods of uncertainty and ambivalence. Effectively I became the determined suitor and Carol, it appeared, needed a lot of convincing in the first three years of our relationship!

From the outset I was quite convinced that this was what God intended for us and I was immediately drawn by the ingredients of her undemanding faithfulness and her single-minded commitment to God. Completely unassuming, she was always totally willing to serve wholeheartedly—as long as it was not on a platform. But her reticence had a lot more to do with her own perceptions about my profile and the warning signs of a busy public ministry. In private conversations it was evident that we were not exactly alike, but in time those differences emerged to complement each other: she was a good listener and I always appeared to have a lot to say; I wrote and she read; I overlooked the obvious details and she was quick to point them out. Very little has changed after eighteen years of marriage! The greatest means of cohesion for us were the common values about God, his work, and the people around us to whom we shared a joint sense of commitment.

Our relationship through those difficult times was a great emotional anchor which helped me to make sense of other things around me. The first four years of marriage closed off the 1970's and took us both into other adventures of parenting and pastoral responsibilities.

Our son was born in 1978 and our daughter in 1982.

Other things began to change around and within me by this stage. A deep sense of purpose began to develop, a sense of direction without details. It often reminded me of the sensation you get when travelling in a car with your eyes closed. You know when the driver is changing direction although you have no idea of your location. Slowly, but very definitely, my direction began to change, but I could not distinguish what God was doing with any clarity.

I remember discussing this on occasions with a good friend, Terrence Caine, who usually smiled very knowingly in support and always managed to choose his words of advice with great care. Terrence had been watching me with keen interest since we first met at a national youth camp when I was nineteen. One evening the phone rang during an EBI staff meeting at our home. It was our national Bishop, Selwyn Arnold, with an invitation to pastor a small church in Mile End, East London. I mentioned it to Terrence who was present at the time; he smiled knowingly.

I was in a state of shock for a week before I felt sufficiently certain to accept the invitation. Having been in church all my life, now, at the age of thirty four, it suddenly became apparent that I had given no serious thought to 'Christian ministry' over and above the opportunities to preach occasionally. My involvement with EBI felt, up to that point, like a congenial accident which had provided me with an opportunity to develop my awareness of God's word after leaving full-time study. Even my work as a probation officer appeared up to that moment to be nothing more than an opportunity to pursue a career I felt was suited to my temperament and general interests.

Time to Change

What actually helped in the decision-making process is very hard to identify. It was certainly no conviction that I was either suitable or capable to undertake the task. By this time I was very much affirmed within my local church, with a very good friend, Ira Brooks, as my local minister; and I held an unofficial role as supporter and friend to a host of younger people who came to regard Carol and me as older siblings. Similarly, I found myself increasingly invited out to preach in other churches and wider conferences such as Leadership '84 and Spring Harvest. But in spite of all these openings there was an inexplicable restlessness which was pacified by this unexpected and terrifying invitation.

One of the most painful experiences of my life was to leave both the church which had been my spiritual home for twenty five years, and the people to whom I owed so much over those years of my long apprenticeship. Our pain in leaving was compensated for only by the inner compulsion to move on. The longest week I can remember was that between leaving and taking up our appointment at the New Testament Church of God in Mile End on September 1st 1985. It seemed as though the entire world was caught up in a conspiracy of silence against me. Those days were filled with passing faces and words which failed to register in my consciousness as I looked behind me with sorrow and before me with unbridled apprehension.

Sunday, September 1st came and we went to our new

church. Mile End was a small congregation with forty five members and a noticeable number of young people. The inaugural morning service went by me as though it were happening to someone else. It was simply too much to take in and emotionally I was still in the farewell service. Reality came at the end of the evening service when one of the deacons, Amos Guthrie, handed me a set of keys for the church building.

Our first five years were both novel and exciting, with all of the challenges and horrors of the learning experience. A new building and a growing church, together with a wider ministry and a full-time job as a probation officer, made life very difficult. It became evident that *something* had to go. Surrendering my work at EBI had simply not been enough. Added to that, the old restless feeling was upon me once again. Light dawned on me during dictation with my seventeen year old secretary one day. Laura had always viewed my hectic lifestyle with incredulity. That day, as we were discussing holidays, she said, 'You take your holidays and go on those Christian things, don't you!' She was right. I took a bold step to take up part-time work and became the first male job-share probation officer in Holloway women's prison. Holloway was hard but, more than ever before, I developed a deep appreciation for concepts like justice and mercy.

My spiritual restlessness was exacerbated by the pain of working with incarcerated women, and I long resisted all overtures to consider senior appointments within the service. It just didn't seem the way forward. Deep within my being I felt that I needed to focus my energy.

It was about that time, at Spring Harvest 1987, that I

met a man with an enormous heart for reconciliation. His name was Philip Mohabir. He told me about his specific burden to see a greater degree of reconciliation between estranged black churches and the wider evangelical church. He explained how this shared vision between senior black Christians and the Evangelical Alliance had led to the launch, in April 1984, of the West Indian Evangelical Alliance, WIEA (now the African and Caribbean Evangelical Alliance ACEA). Philip's relentless persuasion over a number of months resonated with my growing sense of direction, and eventually I left my job-share post to become WIEA's General Secretary in March 1988.

It was only at that point that events of earlier years began to fall into perspective. Increasingly I found that Christian leaders with whom I had studied ten or twelve years previously, and with whom I had had no recent contact, came pouring back into my life. Similarly, the fascination to discover other black churches which had nagged at me all my Christian life now became an integral part of my work.

In providing a reconciliatory ministry between black and white Christians in the United Kingdom, my journey into the black church experience became bound up with my own experience and self-discovery. I became enthralled as I continued to investigate and to articulate the story of our recent history. In my effort to get other Christians to understand the black experience of redemption, I grew to understand more fully many of the things I had felt intuitively in my early years.

Every day was an opportunity to learn, and although the demands of a local church and the WIEA were very heavy, these ministries complemented each other and developed in tandem. The dual work of the local church and the increased profile which came with the work within WIEA and the Evangelical Alliance became absorbing. After three years establishing the structures in both ministries—a team ministry in the church and a growing army of volunteers in ACEA—I was quite confident that the time was right to consolidate the work in both areas. I actually felt as though I now *understood* what I was about.

I was generally 'on a roll'. Life, it seemed, really began at forty, for in my fortieth year I was privileged to become ordained in my denomination, to speak as the main preacher in a national event, and be elected on to the national Executive Council of the New Testament Church of God. To top it all, the local church had given me a surprise birthday party and sent Carol and myself off on a weekend trip to Paris!

It was at this point that something very unusual happened to me when one day I was about to rush out from my home to fulfil yet another appointment. In my bedroom I was held transfixed for what I can only describe as a divine cross-examination. The point was as follows: would I be willing to serve God should he take away all the things I enjoyed? I stood for five or ten minutes and for the first time in many years I was forced to examine my motives carefully. I had never been asked those questions so deeply in my own heart. Those are the sort of enquiries only the individual can truly answer.

It was shortly after that piercing experience that the old, now familiar restlessness seemed to gather momentum. It hardly made any sense. Everything was going so well and so much foundational work had been done. Within a few weeks I understood. The Evangelical Alliance was undergoing a significant restructuring in its senior staff; I was invited to consider a central role on the new and emerging Senior Management Team. To be frank, the invitation seemed totally outrageous, given my own relatively small world and the magnitude of the task. The General Director, Clive Calver, asked me to give it prayerful thought. My first port of call was to my family, who seemed less shocked than I was. I was still in a haze the following day when I discussed it briefly with the Vice-President of ACEA, Melvin Powell, and was given a gentle nudge forward. As my circle of advisors on the subject grew, a very clear and common consensus emerged. I should *definitely* accept the challenge. Rationally, I found it hard to be convinced, but as in previous situations I discovered that my restlessness became satisfied by my increasing willingness to say 'yes'.

Over a number of weeks it was becoming evident that a growing number of close friends and colleagues were quite confident that this was the right direction. I agreed to meet with the General Director and members of the EA Executive. The meeting was conducted late on a Friday afternoon. Afterwards I recall a hasty flight from the office in Kennington to the church in Mile End, where I was scheduled to take a baptismal class, after which I went home to pack for an early morning departure for a conference in Wales.

I hardly had time to think or pray and tumbled through two presentations during the morning and afternoon. The Saturday evening session of the weekend event,

hosted by the Foursquare Church, was particularly ani-
mated. During the closing session of worship a woman
I had never met before walked over to me. She was very
nervous and clearly reticent about doing so. I suggested
that we stepped into the vestibule where it was quieter
and encouraged her again to say whatever she felt she
needed to. 'I see a green light over your head,' she
began. 'The Lord is telling me to tell you that he is about
to extend your ministry. It will include travelling a lot
more than you have done before. The Lord says that you
should go.' I could hardly believe what I was hearing :
but there was more. 'God says to tell you that he has seen
your behaviour all through the years ...'. When eventually she came to a conclusion she was evidently uneasy
about the encounter and still gave the impression of
someone who had invited herself to an 'invitations only'
party. I assured her of the usefulness of what she had
said and she left. I learned later that her name was
Marian Rothuzen, the wife of Paul who supervises the
Foursquare Church in Holland.

I finally agreed to accept the challenge and once
again the restlessness gave way to apprehension. More
than any other single individual, Marian's willingness to
approach me with words she did not fully understand
herself, was a life-transforming intervention which
helped to steer me into the task of co-ordinating evangelical initiatives within the United Kingdom across a
broad spectrum of groups and individuals. The learning
began all over again.

Of course God seldom acts the same way in any given
situation. That vexed question of finding God's purpose
for one's life has no universal patent applicable in all

given circumstances. God must be allowed to be sovereign. My own personal pilgrimage has not been spectacular, but perhaps it may be helpful to others at some point. Most preachers have at some point taught about guidance. Some time ago I had my notes ready to do such a task when I was very pressed to take an alternative route. God did not want a *professional* job that night, he wanted a *personal* one and I was constrained to give my personal testimony as I had never done before! My own experience is that God's guidance often makes more sense in retrospect. It is what I regard as *retrospective revelation*— for whilst most of us are only wise after the events, God is always wise *before* all events.

David is a perfect example of *retrospective revelation*. He, it was said, 'served God's purpose in his generation' (Acts 13:36). That surely was hardly evident before or during the vicissitudes of his long life. But somehow all the success, failures and sins of David's life, with which we so readily identify, failed to derail him from the fixed points of God's plan for him, and so his whole life conspired to serve a greater purpose which became far more intelligible in retrospect.

8

NO BARGAINING WITH GOD

Maizie Smyth

Ballymena, the town nearest to my home in the Braid Valley in Northern Ireland, is famous for its 'good bargains'. Even for goods marked at a reasonable price the residents know there is always room for a further reduction. As a child I heard my parents on many occasions bargaining for good prices for my new shoes or clothes. In my teenage years I was to discover that this was not so in other areas. When on a shopping trip with my elder sister to Belfast, I purchased a pair of shoes. On paying I duly asked the usual Ballymena question as to how much of a reduction I could count on. My blushing sister quickly changed the subject of conversation with the chain store assistant. Once outside I heard in no uncertain terms that one does not bargain with set prices in the big city.

In a similar way, as I listened from an early age to God's word in my Sunday School classes, I knew that the price for being a Christian had already been set. I heard of the need to confess my sin and invite the Lord Jesus to be my Saviour. Throughout these Sunday School classes, even though I heard the way of salvation, never was an opportunity given to do this. I often longed in my heart to trust him. But how? Yes, I heard the way of salvation, but how was I to get from where I was to that way?

During my first year at the local secondary school, a

mission organised by the Faith Mission was conducted in the area. One Sunday evening I went with others to hear God's word being preached. On that particular evening I heard teaching on the words of the Lord Jesus—'I am the door'—and it was very clearly explained that the Lord Jesus, at present an open door to heaven before us, would not always be an open door and that as we heard God's word we should obey it and trust in him. I left the meeting that night knowing that God was calling me to come to him. Perhaps fear of what my friends would say kept me from going to speak with the preacher.

Coming from a farm meant there was always work to be done. It had been arranged earlier that when I returned from the meeting I was to close up the hens for the night. We had perhaps eight houses of free-range hens. Each house had a little trap-door that had to be shut when all the hens were safely inside. As I went to do this work all the hens were in but one. No matter how hard I tried to direct this hen towards that small door, she always seemed defiant and went in the opposite direction. To me this was a clear picture of what was happening in my life. God had put an open door before me, he was calling me, and yet I was just being defiant and going in the opposite direction.

Looking back I suppose, in many ways, I was trying to bargain with God, telling him to take care of me, and that when I grew up I would follow him. But there could be no bargaining. It was a set price—the price of taking him as his word declares. I knew then and there that, as the hen would not stand a chance of survival against the rains, winds and foxes of the dark night, neither could I make it through life on my own. I needed the Lord Jesus, and that evening, in the only way I knew, I asked him to be my Saviour.

Because I decided to keep it all a well-guarded secret, it meant there was little change in my life. I felt that with Jesus as my Saviour I was now ready for heaven should anything happen, but that daily I could live as I pleased. Looking back it is perhaps one of my greatest regrets that I did not know the need to read his word, pray and have fellowship with other believers, and so during my secondary and secretarial education there was no outward change in my life.

Involvement in Christian activities

The hunt for a good job took me to the city. There in Belfast, whilst living at the Presbyterian Hostel, for the first time I met with young Christians who were growing in their Christian faith. They were meeting weekly in a Christian Endeavour group at Berry Street Presbyterian Church and, as a newcomer, I was welcomed into that group.

Not many weeks passed before one of the leaders asked me if I was a Christian. When I said 'yes!' he asked me if I would lead the meeting in prayer in about ten minutes' time—ten minutes of panic as I tried to grapple with phrases which would be suitable for an opening prayer. It was the beginning of involvement in the Christian Endeavour group.

Week by week through Bible studies, discussion groups, and guest speakers I was learning what it meant to be a Christian—not an outward show for others to see but an inward relationship with the living Lord. His word was becoming more and more meaningful as I took time for personal Bible study and prayer. Answers to prayer brought encouragement to be bold and to speak to others of him. With Christian Endeavour's local outreach and missionary activities came opportunities to testify of Christ and his work in my life. As I listened to missionaries from other lands speak of the work they were involved in, more and more my eyes were opened to the needs of the world. I could be involved in meeting the need through praying and giving.

The Unevangelised Fields Mission leader, Rev. Joe Wright, realised that many front-line battles are won through prayer in home prayer groups. He gave us opportunity to fight in these battles through a prayer group he organised, and the concerns of those serving in other lands became our concerns. It was thrilling to meet with missionaries on their visits home and to hear first-hand how God was answering our prayers.

Paul had urged the Thessalonians to pray without ceasing for him; how much more did the missionaries in Brazil, Zaire and Ivory Coast need it now! Men, women, boys and girls in these lands were accepting the claims of Jesus Christ and trusting him as their Saviour, churches were growing and reaching out to tell others of him. To be involved in praying for these churches and finan-cially supporting missionaries was indeed a privilege as well as an education in beginning to trust the Lord. Missionary meetings always left me with the desire to do more for my Lord, a desire which I didn't directly re-spond to.

On one occasion the need of the children in our own city was presented. Many of them were growing up in godless homes with no one to teach them the word of

God. After that particular meeting I spoke with the missionary and offered to help whichever way I could during the week. I still travelled to my home every weekend where I was now teaching in the local Sunday School. That offer resulted in training classes on how to teach God's word to boys and girls and also studies in some basic Bible doctrines. 'Your word is a lamp to my feet and a light for my path' (Psalm 119:105) certainly became true as I delved into his word in these classes, preparing to teach others.

Life was exciting! I was living it to the full and enjoying sharing that joy with many others.

Being the owner of an ancient Ford Anglia car meant I could come and go as I liked; and yet it was so useful in transporting others to meetings, outings etc. So I reasoned that most of the work my small car did was for the Lord and that he would not mind if I had a 'decent car'. I was bargaining with God in a silent way which I was sure he would understand. Never did it cross my mind that he was interested in my whole life and what I did with it. I was more or less giving him the leftovers. So I started saving seriously to buy a brand new Mini.

For a couple of years my holidays involved me in a local camp. This was not financially draining although physically it was. Up to 50 children under canvas in Northern Irish weather (rain from start to finish!) doesn't exactly leave one feeling 'well rested'. That tiredness, however, could not be compared with the joy of teaching these children the truth of God's word and counselling some of them in their desire to follow him. I learned that young children can trust the Lord and become witnesses for him as they grow in his grace.

The 'troubles' were just commencing in Ireland. Our weekly children's class was in a predominantly Roman Catholic area where it was known that many of the parents were involved in the 'activities'. What opportunities on my doorstep to teach God's word and to see him at work! We had about a 2% Protestant presence in that meeting of well over one hundred children.

I remember on one occasion about thirty boys coming into the meeting, each of them eating a banana. The fruit lorry had parked outside the local shop. While the driver confirmed the shop order with the shopkeeper inside, his fruit was disappearing on the street.

Practical lessons needed to be taught, but greater still were the claims of God on our lives. Only eternity will reveal what work was done through the faithful witness of the Belfast City Missioner and his team.

Challenged as to my priorities
Realising that the office where I worked was a mission field, I sought to live there for the Lord. While it was good to see the other members of staff respecting my Christian beliefs and not using swear words in my presence, I prayed that I would see more than that, even a hunger to know about God.

The local city mission church had a special week of meetings. I invited several of my colleagues to attend one evening. Thrilled that three agreed to come, I prayed much that the Lord would speak to them clearly. I was to be surprised. The text that evening was from Luke 12:15: 'Watch out! Be on your guard against all kinds of greed; a man's life does not consist in the abundance of possessions.' The preacher explained how we can gather material goods to ourselves and spend so much time thinking about them that we have no time for God, even though he demands first place. I had an uncomfortable niggling feeling about my savings for my car, but bargained or reasoned that it was for 'the Lord's work'. I was most disappointed that none of my friends seemed moved by the preaching of God's word, but certainly my heart was not at rest.

Over the next two days I heard further sermons on the same subject. So, after the Sunday evening service, in the attic bedroom of my flat which I shared with two other Christian girls, I sorted out my financial needs and responsibilities in the light of God's word. All I had was his. How could I have been so naive as to 'save' it for my own use in days to come? I had not been tithing in the way I ought. That evening saw me sharing my savings with the various mission groups with which I was involved and only retaining what I needed for my written financial commitments.

One of these was a holiday a fortnight later at a Child Evangelism Fellowship conference in the first week of June. Little did I know that night that God was only beginning to prod me in a way which would transform all my plans for future days.

The conference proved to be a week of blessing through the Bible readings and missionary presentations, not to mention the rich fellowship. One day at lunch, a missionary I had never met before said to me, 'If God ever calls you to Bible School, go to the BTI.' As an ex-student of the Glasgow Bible Training Institute perhaps he thought he was their publicity agent!

During that week the need for workers seemed to

grow bigger and bigger. Coupled with that was the continual question in my mind: 'Am I really doing what God wants me to do?' I was quite sure I was. Yet was God prodding me to move on? With lots of friends around at the conference, I made sure I didn't have too much time on my own to think about these serious things.

For the return trip home on the Liverpool to Belfast boat I was on my own and on that Saturday night crossing I slept little. This was not because the sea was rough, but because God was telling me that I should go to Bible School. Was I willing to give my all for him? He had given his all for me and yet I only wanted to be 'part-time' for God. My Ballymena culture was showing itself as I bargained with God, but I ought to have known he has the final say. Weary and wanting to sleep I finally said, 'O.K., Lord, I will go to Bible School if you put me out of my flat or my job.' That to me was the final bargain price.

I shared a house with two other girls. The elderly owner of the house depended on us for almost everything from shopping to housekeeping jobs. Therefore I felt I was on safe ground asking that we would be put out of the house! No way would that woman dispense with her three free 'home helps'! I had worked for nearly ten years in a local government office and was now in a good position there. I knew my job was safe. With this 'safe bargain', I slept until we reached Belfast harbour in the early morning.

I shared the holiday excitement with my two flat mates but without mention of God's dealings with me over the week or indeed the previous night. As we exchanged news, one of them said, 'Things have changed here a little since you left. The elderly owner of the house downstairs believes it's time to sell her house and move to her son in England; she has given us one month to look for another house!' I was speechless, to say the least! God had certainly come out best in that bargain.

Bible College

The next few weeks were exciting. I had, as it were, put God to the test and he had won. Now I must follow his leading. It had to be Bible School; but where and how? I had all the excuses at my finger tips. I only work in an office—that is not a job for the mission field. I have no money left and fees at Bible School are high. Should I save for a year and then go? No, I had promised I would go this year if God ... and he had answered. Now I must do as he had asked. I sent for applications to three Bible Schools, including the BTI.

As replies came back, it seemed everything pointed towards the Bible Training Institute in Glasgow. One evening I started to read a short biography of W. P. Nicholson, a famous but rather uncouth Irish preacher. From what I had heard of his style of preaching I assumed he had not had any formal Bible School training. I was most surprised to read that he had in fact been to the BTI! It seemed that this Bible School was cropping up all over the place.

That night as I read God's word it said very clearly: 'I will instruct you and teach you in the way you should go; I will counsel you and watch over you.' I was definitely to go and he was leading.

My application was sent to the BTI. One week later they asked me to come for interview. If I was to leave my job at the end of August I had no days of leave left. To go for an interview would be difficult. I talked with the college staff by telephone and they said they would be in touch. I gave a sigh of relief, knowing that without an interview I would never be accepted.

The college authorities were in touch a few days later with the following news: 'You are accepted to begin at BTI at the beginning of September. We will interview you on your arrival here. We note, however, that you have no money for fees but you say that you have faith. If you have faith for September you can have it for August and we are therefore asking you to forward one term's fees (£125) before the end of August.'

This letter was received on the last Monday morning in July. What was I to do? I didn't have enough for one week's fees because of God's dealings with me and my money only a couple of months earlier.

I needed to give in my notice at work. No one had any idea what had been happening to me over recent weeks. I took time that morning in work to type my letter of resignation and to give it to our director. Within half an hour, I was in his office trying to persuade him I would not turn back and would not consider putting off Bible School for one year. It is amazing the many holes we are given to escape through! By lunchtime it seemed the canteen was buzzing with the news that this 'piece of office furniture' was leaving. I suppose many saw me as a career person and could not imagine me moving on.

A Christian man who worked in another department asked me to stop by and see him in his office after lunch. As I sat down across the desk from him, this sad man explained how God had called his own son to go to Bible School, but that he had stopped him and today his son was far from God. This man was carrying the burden of being a stumbling block for the Lord. He said, 'It seems God is giving me a second chance. God has laid on my heart today to give you this. You know what you can use it for.'

He had given me a plain white envelope with my name on it. I thanked him, returned to my office and quickly opened the envelope to see what was inside it— a cheque for £125. I wept with joy as I realised how small I was trying to make God fit into my plans when his plans were far greater than I could ever think of. 'For I know the plans I have for you,' declares the Lord, 'plans to prosper you and not to harm you, plans to give you hope and a future' (Jeremiah 29:11).

My mind was not on 'office matters' that afternoon but only on how great my God was. Now I could send my first term's fees off to BTI.

> How good is the God we adore,
> Our faithful unchangeable Friend,
> Whose love is as great as his power,
> And knows neither measure nor end!'

The Lord with whom I had bargained that Saturday night on the Liverpool boat certainly was bigger than ever I had imagined.

Telling my parents and friends of my call to go to Bible School proved easier than I thought. The Lord had prepared each of them to receive the news. Isn't it great that he is in charge of every situation? I was learning that I shouldn't bargain with him as he always 'won'.

On saying goodbye to my friends in CEF and

Unevangelised Fields Mission prayer groups, I vowed that I would not keep in touch with the leaders as I suspected they would try and 'net me' for their mission. I didn't want to be led by them but by God who had called me to Bible School.

September soon came and I found about thirty five other new students in the same situation as myself—not knowing which direction to turn in the 'old castle' (as it was affectionately called). How would we ever cope with lectures, homework etc. I had not been in school for over ten years. Would I ever adapt? Some lectures seemed easier than others ... but it was the difficult ones I prayed over the most. Living in dormitories brought its own rules and regulations and its encouragements and discouragements. I soon discovered that my sheltered Christian environment of Northern Ireland was being tested on all sides. Not only should I say, 'It's right to do such and such a thing,' but I had to know why.

As part of the Bible School course each student was assigned to practical outreach. I was sent to work with the Glasgow Medical Mission in the Gorbals. Enquiries brought raised eyebrows at the mention of the Gorbals and other comments like, 'It will be tough there.' The new pastor for the Medical Mission was being installed on the Saturday, so our four-member team was invited along to the service. The following Monday evening we would be introduced and would spend time working out our programme and praying together.

The new pastor was Bill Gilvear. As he shared his testimony, I could not believe what I was hearing. He had just come home from Zaire with the UFM, of all missions, and I was to work with him! So much for my thought of keeping clear of all links with UFM!

We had many opportunities of sharing God's word with the folks in the new flats in and around the Gorbals; and Bill Gilvear proved to be very helpful and encouraging in the work there. At the end of each evening's visitation, around a cup of tea we listened to more of Bill's experiences in Zaire. As a team we had great times of fellowship and prayer and Bill was interested in God's leading for each of us.

Time at BTI was flying. After spending two of my summers working as a summer missionary with C.E.F. in Southern Ireland, I would have been very happy to return there to work full-time. There were many reasons for this, so that I thought I could easily bargain with God. In Southern Ireland I would use English as a language, would not be far from home, knew most of the folk who were already in the team etc. When would I ever learn?

Call to Zaire

One Monday evening after our Gorbals visitation, Bill asked me if I was going to the UFM missionary weekend starting on Friday. I said 'No.' He guessed correctly that I did not have enough money to go. As we were leaving he prayed, 'Lord, if you want Maizie to go the UFM missionary weekend let her receive money for it from Belfast tomorrow.' It was now 10.30 pm and that was definitely something he couldn't fix!

I felt 'safe'; there would be no money. But next morning I had a letter from a lady in Belfast containing the exact amount of money needed for the weekend. She simply said, 'The Lord has shown me you will need this.' How could I not go to the missionary weekend?

It was there I heard all about the need in Zaire. Psalm 32:8 kept coming back to me and there was a real struggle going on in my heart. No, I could never go to Zaire—I was going to Southern Ireland. I had not made mention of this to anyone but the Lord.

For the next week the struggle continued daily. In my bargaining I lined up all my 'excuses' before the Lord. At school I was anything but good at English. If I couldn't speak my own language correctly, how would I ever learn another language? Zaire needed doctors, nurses and teachers and I was none of these. No, I could not go to Zaire. The list of excuses was endless, but God was patient.

The missions lecture that Friday morning just 'happened' to be on Zaire, not by someone from UFM but from another mission. I didn't get too much from his statistically-loaded lecture, but his ending went something like this: 'You may be saying to God that you are neither a doctor, teacher or nurse and therefore cannot go to Zaire. Today Zaire needs those who know they are called by God to share his word with folk from all levels of the community.'

I heard nothing more. It was the largest bomb that had ever sounded in the classroom for me at the BTI. I beat a hasty retreat to my room where I cried my eyes out, realising God was indeed calling me to Zaire. Yes, he had won the bargaining process yet again. His word that afternoon was, 'Be strong and courageous. Do not be afraid or terrified because of them, for the Lord your God goes with you; he will never leave you nor forsake you.' What more could I ask?

The next few months of 1976 flew past in the process

of completing mission application forms, doing final exams at BTI, going to the CEF Summer Institute for three months. There I praised God for his clear call to me to serve in Zaire, because I found that many folk thought it was natural that I would go with CEF to Southern Ireland. My call was being tested before I ever went out to Zaire.

There were UFM interviews on my return at the end of the summer and then a candidates' course in November. This was two weeks of 'them' getting to know 'us' and 'us' getting to know 'them'. The candidates shared great times together, learning about the mission, exploring London in our spare time and learning how to live with one another.

Jill Thompstone had recently returned from Zaire. She was one of the hostesses for the course, as well as giving various lectures on missionary life. Her slides gave a clear picture of life in Zaire. As I listened to all she had done there I again started bargaining with God. 'Lord, you've got it all wrong. If it is missionaries like Jill you want in Zaire, then I am not the one. I am not capable of doing any of these things.' Again as I wrestled in prayer, it was his word that spoke very clearly to me: 'You are my servant; I have chosen you and have not rejected you. So do not fear, for I am with you; do not be dismayed, for I am your God. I will strengthen you and help you; I will uphold you with my righteous right hand' (Isaiah 41:9, 10). God's word was so personal and so practical that my fears were gone. He had called *me* and I was not to look around and be envious of others. Final interviews over, I was pronounced 'a missionary candidate for Zaire'.

A few months later I was back in school, but this time in the French Alps to study French. The train journey was horrific as I did not know one word of French and no one seemed to know any English. Only the Lord knows how I arrived at the centre where he was to teach me many things during the next eight months—and it wasn't just the French language. I had dreaded going there and yet they were very happy months of rich fellowship with the mainly American student body.

Phonetic classes would have been lowest on my list of favourites. One Monday morning in March the teacher decided it would be the day to put me through my paces. It seemed I couldn't produce any of the noises the way the French did. At mid-morning break I left the classroom feeling very discouraged and wondering if I would ever say anything with the correct accent. Surely there would be some good letters in the postbox to brighten my day.

Yes, there was one. As I read it in my own room I found it was another bombshell. 'We at UFM regret to tell you of our decision to withdraw from working with the church in the Zaire field. This will mean that you will not be able to go to Zaire as originally planned.' I don't think I read any more of that letter. There were floods of tears.

I spent the rest of the day in my room trying to come to terms with all this. Had I made a *big* mistake? Yet God's word was a solid foundation. He had given me that word and I would stand on it. 'Lord, what is your word in this situation?' I spent a long time reading and praying and reasoning it all out. 'These are the words of him who is holy and true, who holds the key of David. What he opens no-one can shut, and what he shuts no-one can open .... See, I have placed before you an open door that no-one can shut. I know that you have little strength' (Revelation 3:7, 8).

Joy flooded my soul as I saw that this was just another hill I had to climb. The great thing was that I was walking in his way for me. The Lord would take me to Zaire. And he did, to work in the joint Theological School at Bunia.

God's open door
Some twenty years previously, a Theological School had been started at Banjwade, near Kisangani. Because of political unrest, difficulties in travel, as well as other reasons, it was decided to move it nearer to the Uganda border. Today it is located in Bunia. It had been the vision of Rev. H. Jenkinson, one of the founder missionaries of UFM, and was now a joint effort of five missionary societies. UFM informed me of the possibility of working there until the door opened into the Kisangani region.

It was only five years since God had started prodding me about going to Bible School and now here I was settling into life in Zaire. One would think that with Bible School and language school training behind me, it was now time to 'work'. I was ready, but I discovered that the folk I would be teaching knew very little French. I would have to learn their language, Swahili. They were the wives of the Bible school students together with the young people of Bunia. To communicate God's word to them I needed, it seemed, to start all over again. At the BTI, I had bargained with God saying that I couldn't learn another language. Yet here I was starting out on yet another one!

Within two months of starting to learn Swahili I was back in Bunia teaching in the school. There were lots of tears as I struggled with the language in preparation of lessons, adjusting to a new culture and a different approach to all aspects of life. I praise him for the laughs in class as someone explained how I had just used the wrong word. I confused angels and green beans. When telling the Christmas story the children were in fits of laughter as I told of the green beans filling the heavens to praise God. It was all a learning process.

As I began to communicate more easily and to understand what was being said, it was a thrill to listen to the Bible School students and their wives tell of how God had brought them to Bunia. Many had travelled by canoe and by lorry for weeks or even months just to study God's word. As I listened to them I discovered that many had been bargaining too. 'Lord, who will care for our family?' 'Lord, how will we get there? ' 'Lord, who will pay our fees?' Yet God's word was the rock on which they were building.

My job description was to help in the training of the pastors' wives at the Theological Seminary in Bunia and to be part of the local Christian Education team. Being trained in children's work I joined the child evangelism team working in Bunia and surrounding district.

A village seminar
Travel was difficult as I had no vehicle of my own. Our first trip in a loaned vehicle was an 'experience'. As it was forest country we spent our first day using hatchets and a saw to clear the road of fallen trees.

The final straw came three miles from the church.

There, in the road, was a mud hole in which we could have buried the vehicle. With no experience of Zairian roads I tried to go around it but, alas, got well and truly stuck. The wheels of the vehicle were no longer visible. How would we ever get out of the hole? It was too late at this stage to wish for an electric winch. We had nothing but a shovel and a hoe. Darkness was approaching and so was the village population.

Our dilemma becomes their blessing. They know we won't want to dig, and that we will enlist their help at an agreed price. They are on the winning side as we are *stuck*. I've come to the land of bargaining. God doesn't make any mistakes with our backgrounds either. Two hours later, and with a lighter purse, we are on our way.

The village folk are jubilant to see us. A storm is brewing overhead so we're advised to take our baths speedily. Famous last words! As it is my first time in the village I get the privilege of being first to the bathroom. A few bamboo sticks form a circle with banana leaves firmly secured to them. Underfoot is another layer of banana leaves. It's the best colour coordinated bathroom possible!

A hurricane lamp is suspended from a bamboo stick but it has only half a globe. The lamp is essential as the moon is not yet up. A bucket of hot water, a bar of soap, and a vine tied across the 'bathroom' (to hang up one's clothes) completes the facilities. I strip off and slosh some of the lovely hot water over my body. When did a 'bath' ever feel so good ... we had had a hard day's work. I was midway through soaping my body when the soap slipped out of my hand and slid somewhere into my 'carpet' of banana leaves. Now to look for it. I was well into my search when a gust of wind came and took advantage of the half globe. Out went the light! I never did find the soap, I didn't get the lovely bath I was anticipating but only a quick rinse, and then I dried and struggled into my dirty clothes again. I certainly had a lot to learn about village life.

We spent the evening huddled around a few burning sticks as the storm raged outside. At bedtime I soon discovered their beds were very different. They were bow-shaped ... low in the middle and up at both ends. Suffice it to say that after trying to sleep, my hump didn't fit into the hump of the bed. Very kindly the village folk made a new mattress for me—old flour bags sewn together and filled with new cut grass. The first half hour was very comfortable, but then the grass fleas found that my blood was very tasty and so we fought the whole night long.

These 'discomforts' were nothing to be compared with the joy of teaching some fifty Sunday School teachers who had walked for miles just to be at that three-day course. As we taught, discussed and listened it was evident that God was at work in our midst. A Sunday School teacher of many years wasn't sure if Jesus had really come into her heart, and so each week would invite him in again. A young man had been so involved in witchcraft that he was tormented by fear that 'it' would return. Sitting around camp fires in the evenings we answered questions from God's word.

In Zaire these times of questions were always full. As I learned more of the culture, I soon realised that many of these questions were coming from the pastors. Why? In the dark they were not embarrassed to ask questions.

They had left Bible School many years ago and had no textbooks to help them in their studies. How important God's word is in our lives! It is only as I read and meditated on it myself that I could aid these folk who were crying out for help.

God had surely brought me to Zaire. I was finding out day by day that he was going before me.

On Monday morning at 8 am we started our three-day seminar in another village. In the morning sunshine the village sounds filled the air. Soon we heard the goat being pulled towards the place of its execution. That was to be our 'meat' for the next three days. The Christians there had saved hard to be able to afford this goat.

Three hours later, wailing started in the village and soon we heard that the pastor's mother, who had been ill for some weeks, had just died. We could not continue our seminar nor could we stay, as soon the 'greater family' would all appear and would need to be housed and fed. We had a quick committee meeting and it was decided we should leave and return on Thursday.

By 11 am that Thursday we all wondered what was happening. The smell that permeated the village was anything but pleasant and it even reached the church. The precious goat had been kept and we were to be served it for lunch for the next three days. The custom is that the visitor's plate is always prepared. You cannot serve yourself. How was I ever to eat the four ounces of 'rotten meat' on my plate? Would I cause offence if I didn't eat it? Would I be sick if I ate it? Many thoughts went through my mind, but I knew I had to eat it. I cut it up in small portions and swallowed it like medicine.

I had done my part and the Lord certainly did his in

preventing me from being sick. It was only years later that I discovered to have refused would have meant a total end to my teaching in that area. If I was not prepared to eat their 'delicacies', who did I think I was in trying to teach them God's word.

The teacher-training seminar programme was full. There were so many villages asking us to come and teach, yet I had to be present at Bunia during term time. Local Sunday School helped me to understand the Zairian child and through this, God blessed his word as we shared it weekly with many children.

Home Bible studies

As we held teacher-training classes in Bunia it became evident that most of the teachers wanted more training in God's word. I opened my home on Thursday evenings for Bible study but stipulated that each Christian must bring an unsaved person. My little living room was packed as thirty or more people crowded in each week. As the local pastor led the study we discovered many things. I was learning a lot about how the Zairian relates to God's word. Many were bargaining just as I had done and each week we would keep coming back to 'taking God at his word'.

One day the Number 2 political man of our area asked me if he could come to the Bible study. I was delighted and assured him that he would be very welcome. He and his wife were soon to be regular attenders. Months passed and we broke up for a week for Christmas holidays.

On Christmas Day, two local immigration officials came for my help. They were suffering from malaria, a very common occurrence in Zaire. Could I supply them with malarial treatment? They knew I had the tablets so, unofficially, I gave them some.

Sunday was Boxing Day, a quieter day. About 4 pm a large car pulled up in front of my house. I immediately recognised the 'chief medical officer' together with the Number 1 political man from our area. I greeted them at the door and offered them a place to sit in my living room. After the customary greetings, Number 1 said something like this: 'We have a very serious problem in our town and you are the cause of it.' I had learned by now that one goes slowly with problems so I excused myself and went to make a cup of tea. The problem would not be so bad over tea. In the kitchen my mind was in a whirl. The doctor was with him so that meant one of the immigration folk must be very ill. I had given medicine and I was not approved to do so. I was in deep trouble. My thoughts ran riot.

I served the tea, and then Number 1 started on the problem. 'Last Thursday evening someone from the World Bank came to our town. As I had a previous engagement I asked my assistant, Number 2, to entertain him. He told me he had a previous engagement too and could not change it. When I enquired as to what his engagement was, he explained that each Thursday he comes here for Bible study. My question to you is: Why did you not think it necessary to invite me to this Bible study? Don't you know that I am Number 1 in this town and I need God's word more than anyone else? And here is the regional doctor and surely he needs God's word too?'

I was flabbergasted. This was no problem but a great

blessing as here was Number 1 asking to be taught God's word! Two weeks later we had started another Bible study for the 'elite' of Bunia, this time in French taught by pastor colleagues from the Theological School.

What opportunities and what blessings we saw as God's word took root in people's lives! For instance, an ex-priest declared openly, 'Tonight I see God's word as I've never seen it before. It is the living word.' The promise, 'I will instruct and teach you in the way you should go; I will counsel you and watch over you', was proving to be true each day of my life.

I knew God had called me to the Kisangani area of Zaire, but was very happy in Bunia at the joint Theological Seminary. He started prodding again. 'Lord, the door is still closed. The mission will not return there until there has been reconciliation in the church.' It was to be a prod for prayer. Was I really praying for the church in that area?

New location
Furlough came. I knew I would not return to Bunia but to Kisangani. How? It looked impossible. Four months before the end of furlough some missionary colleagues said God was calling them to Kisangani. Things began to happen quickly and within four months the way was clear for the team of four to proceed to Kisangani where the church had been reconciled. This was the condition for the mission to start working there again. By the end of the year the original team of four was halved due to medical problems, and yet despite the *many* disappointments of the move God's word was the rock for us.

Another single girl and I started work there, but

within six months my co-worker was on her way home due to sickness. Would the mission allow me to stay there on my own? His word assured me, 'My Presence will go with you, and I will give you rest.' God has said, 'Never will I leave you; never will I forsake you. So we say with confidence, "The Lord is my helper; I will not be afraid. What can man do to me?" ' 'Our competence comes from God.' Again it was not bargaining with God, but taking him at his word.

Political unrest had caused most of the other missionaries to remain at home after an enforced evacuation. As I was treasurer of the Kisangani church, as well as teaching in the Bible school, I knew my absence would cause greater hardship. Any aid from the West could not be touched unless I was there to handle the cheques etc. So I found myself as the only Protestant missionary in Kisangani. Others came and left due to the instability.

The unrest continued. During one particularly bad day in December 1992, shooting had started at 3 am. By 6 am, the streets were crowded with soldiers venting their anger over the economic situation by firing live rounds into the air. We all stayed indoors except for those dear Christian brothers and sisters who came to make sure I was all right. What love they have shown me!

About 1 pm five soldiers arrived at our gate. The enclosed yard of our house was a refuge for my landrover. One soldier asked his colleague in Lingala, 'Is there a vehicle in that yard?' All other vehicles in Kisangani had been commandeered but mine was still safe. I watched the soldiers from behind closed curtains and was praying, 'Lord, put a hedge around us.' The other soldier's reply was clear, 'A vehicle! What would you do with that? You cannot even drive!'

As the soldiers continued their shooting throughout the night and next day my heart was at peace with God. He had called me here, he had brought me here and he would keep me here in his own way. A text-card received from friends the previous week was so true. It read, 'Do not fear, for I am with you; do not be dismayed, for I am your God' (Isaiah 41:10). God was surely teaching me through various circumstances that his word was the rock.

Even though I had been in Zaire fifteen years, I was still meeting with many new experiences. Was I really learning to listen to his voice through his word and prayer? He often reminds me that 'when he has brought out all his own, he goes on ahead of them, and his sheep follow him because they know his voice' (John 10:4).

Listening to his voice and then obeying is the key. But when will I ever learn that? I seem to slip into bargaining with him so easily and I should know by now that he will have his way. 'I will instruct you and teach you in the way you should go; I will counsel you and watch over you' (Psalm 32:8).

9

BUT WHAT ABOUT ME?

Geoffrey Grogan

Psalm 107 is a wonderfully graphic psalm. Its great theme is the unfailing love of God and the psalmist tells a number of stories in illustration of his theme.

One is about wanderers in a desert, another about folk facing the ravages of mortal disease, another about prisoners languishing in a dungeon, while yet another pictures mariners trying to control a ship that is buffeted by huge waves. Each faced apparently impossible situations and then experienced the marvellous intervention of the God of all grace. Then, in the final verse, the psalmist addresses the reader with these words: 'Whoever is wise, let him heed these things and consider the great love of the Lord.'

The theme of the present book is the faithfulness of God to Christians who are seeking his will for their life and service. What then is wisdom for us? Like the readers of Psalm 107, we need to reflect on specific stories of his dealings with people and learn something from them. We should consider what the Bible teaches and how these stories illustrate that teaching.

If in fact we are concerned to know and do God's will, there are certain actions we need to take and certain attitudes we should have.

1. Actions we should take

One of the most persistent mistakes Christians make about guidance is to imagine that it requires them to be passive. Just sit back and wait for it to come! But trusting God does not mean inactivity. A few verses taken at random from Hebrews 11 should soon dispel that delusion.

What then should we do?

First and foremost, we should expose ourselves as fully as we can to the teaching of Scripture.

This must always come first. The Bible is of supreme importance in everything connected with the Christian life.

More important than Christ? More important than the Holy Spirit? After all Christ is God, the Holy Spirit is God, and the Bible is a book. All three statements are true, of course, and yet the third is misleading when it is added to the other two in a sentence like that.

The only Christ we know is the Christ of Scripture and he placed the seal of his authority on it. He did this by the way he used the Old Testament, quoting it as authoritative and showing in his own life how seriously he viewed all that it taught. He did it also as he spent many hours teaching the truths of the gospel to his apostles, truths they and those close to them would later communicate as they wrote the pages of the New Testament. We should not drive a wedge between Christ and the Bible. Scripture is really Christ's address to us.

The Bible is also intimately related to the Holy Spirit. It was he who inspired both the prophets and the apostles in their communication of God's truth. In every age of the Church's life, and never more so than today, Christians have needed a test by which to assess what appears to be the prompting of the Holy Spirit. We certainly need that, as it is possible for us to make mistakes in discerning the Spirit's guidance. In Scripture he has given us his own means of testing any movements in our own hearts.

A person's authority is usually mediated to us through what he or she says. If then the Bible is God's word, he addresses us with authority as we read it.

Is the Bible then more important than prayer? After all, we are completely dependant on God to show us the way and we need to come to him in prayer to seek that guidance. Certainly, but remember that it is the Bible that shows us both the need to pray and also how to pray. For the Christian, prayer is a responsive activity. God speaks in his word; we respond in prayer.

There are in fact many means of grace, which are really channels God uses to show us his will and his way, means like prayer, Christian fellowship, the ordinances or sacraments, and so on; but the Bible is primary, as it is the Bible that tells us about all the others and how to use them.

There God shows us his great purposes and we see how the lives of individual godly men and women fit into those purposes. Here we learn the great principles by which God gives shape to the lives of his people.

Was there ever such a varied book as the Bible? It contains history, biography, law, meditations, sermons, letters and a number of other literary forms. This is immensely helpful, for not only does it constantly stimulate our interest, but it means that the truth comes to us in so many different ways, one reinforcing another.

Sometimes it comes in forceful imperatives, at other

times in stories about people, and at still others in great affirmations about God and ourselves. Often it appeals to the imagination; at other times it presents powerful arguments to our minds, and there are passages capable of moving us deeply.

Live imaginatively in the Bible world and you will hear the call of God as it came to many of its characters: to Noah the ark-maker, to Abraham the emigrant, to Moses the leader and lawgiver, to Nehemiah the builder, to prophets like Amos, Isaiah and Jeremiah and to apostles such as Peter and Paul.

Read Deuteronomy, the Psalms and Proverbs and you will find many promises of God's guidance to his people.

Read the epistles of Paul and you will learn the great principles of Christian living which form the foundation of all God's dealings with us today.

Best of all, read the story of Christ himself, not only his exhortations to live and walk in the light of God and his word, but also to see his own awareness that he was walking in God's ways and that the timing of the events of his life and death was fulfilling a Divine plan.

It was not only the well-known people who knew and experienced the guidance of God. We can learn so much from the story of Abraham's servant told in Genesis 25 and it is interesting to discover that there are references in the New Testament to a doctor (Colossians 4:14), a lawyer (Titus 3:13) and a city's director of public works (Romans 16:23), all Christians and all serving Christ in their professions.

Even more important than guidance about specific decisions is the Bible's revelation of what God is like and the help it gives us as we seek to develop a godly lifestyle. There needs to be commitment to Christ and also openness to God in prayer and in Bible reading. There should also be fellowship with the people of God in a local church. This is all taken for granted, or should be.

You will have noticed time and again in the testimonies of those whose stories appear in this book how important the Bible was to them. Donald Bridge set himself a study course on the whole Bible, a course which occupied him for many years. Paul Harvey followed the very demanding and yet deeply satisfying programme of reading devised by Murray McCheyne. Several of them had periods of study within the discipline of a college. Taken as a whole, they reveal a great appetite for the word of God. Is it any wonder then that they received guidance from him?

It is this exposure to the whole Bible and the concern to live in the light of it which enables us to grow in wisdom so that when the need for special guidance comes we have been prepared in advance for this. Mary Mealyea has some helpful things to say about this.

Sometimes guidance from Scripture comes from a particular passage. Maizie Smyth and Neil Innes, among others, tell us how God used specific verses in this way.

Such passages should never of course be understood in a way that is alien to their context. To do this would be to mishandle the Scriptures, not to interpret them. If you make a passage mean something quite different from what it signified originally, you are really making up your own guidance and twisting Scripture to justify it. There can be many descriptions of such a process, but 'hearing God's voice' is not one of them.

There should be some kind of real parallel between the situation contemplated in the Biblical passage and your own, so that there is a principle of analogy operating. This is because God is consistent. No two situations are totally alike, but it is God who does not change and who is always true to himself as he has been revealed in Christ and in the Scriptures.

A text of Scripture is sometimes treated as if it is an omen, predicting in some way (for good or ill) the kind of day a person will have. Worst of all is to try to use a text to induce something to happen, almost like a magic spell. Such procedures, even if employed by Christians, owe far more to paganism than they do to Biblical Christianity. If however we are coming to an increasing understanding of God's ways by regular reading and study of Scripture, we soon find his providence to be at work in and through the system of reading we are using. Passages that have a clear relevance for our life today begin to glow with new significance, and such occurrences are not isolated events but part of the general pattern of life.

Read the story of our Lord's temptations as recorded in Matthew 4 or Luke 4. You will note not only that he answers all the temptations from the Old Testament but that all three quotations are from one section (chapters 6-8) of Deuteronomy. Could these chapters have been the basis of his own personal meditation during this period?

In fact, no part of the Old Testament could have been more apt, for in this section of Deuteronomy God is teaching his people, Israel, encamped just outside the Promised Land, what he expected of them when they had entered it. They were in need of guidance as to their corporate lifestyle. There is a real parallel therefore between Israel's situation then and that of Jesus as he faced major issues just before the commencement of his ministry.

Really, the first principle the Bible teaches us is to read, study and obey the Bible!

The next principle, like all the others, is in fact derived from the Bible itself. It is that we should cultivate prayerful daily dependence on God.

The Christian life is a life of faith, nourished by prayer. We need to strengthen through practice that attitude of dependence on God which began at our conversion. To trust Christ for personal salvation is of crucial importance, but it is in fact simply the beginning of a life in which prayerful dependence is to embrace the whole of our existence.

This means that the routine of our everyday existence will be committed to him just as definitely as the special events of life in which we are more conscious of needing to understand his will.

We should not treat God as a provision for emergencies. In fact, we should not treat him as a means to an end at all. Our place is to respond to him. This means allowing him to address his word to us, and then giving our wholehearted assent to it in faith, obedience and worship.

Begin each day with joyful surrender to his will, and let this good start be the dominant characteristic of the day as its hours proceed. If you read the Book of Nehemiah, you will find that this man of God often lifts up his heart to God in a brief 'telegram' prayer in which he seeks protection or encouragement or guidance. He was so aware of God as the constant background to his life that he could easily move in and out of that background and be in conscious touch with the Lord.

Joel Edwards writes of a steady awareness of God. See too how Maizie Smyth lifted up her heart to God at a time of special need and saw the vehicle that was so vital to her work protected from those who might otherwise have taken it.

It is of course very important that personal concerns should not put our prayer-life out of focus. Worshipping God for his great deeds and for all that he is in himself must have first place. Only as we see him as he is will our hearts be drawn out in that surrender to him without which any talk of seeking God's will is meaningless.

Then there should be time for intercession for others. It is so easy to imagine that my life and my concerns are of prime importance—and so arrogant! Others too need the Lord's encouragement, his guidance, his protection, his power, and if we have promised to pray for them, that promise needs to be fulfilled.

The nurture provided by the local church is a great means of grace, in fact it is a multiple means, for there we are able to hear God's word, to pray, to have fellowship with other Christians and to engage in service in our local community.

Some of our contributors have emphasized this more than others, but it has undoubtedly been a factor in the spiritual development and the shaping of life for each of them. It is not God's plan for any of us that we should 'go it alone', but rather that we should grow up spiritually in close fellowship with other Christians.

Some of the churches where these folk received their initial nurture as Christians must have been very different. To worship in the Highland Presbyterian church in which Neil Innes was reared, to move from there to a Brethren Assembly in north-east England and sit beside Donald Bridge, and then travel south to a service at the Pentecostal church in London to which Joel Edwards belonged, would be to enter three different worlds and to experience three very different Christian subcultures. Yet in each of them there was the faithful preaching of the word of God and loving concern for the spiritual welfare of people.

What place has the advice of other people in our lives as Christians?

It may be quite considerable. After all, although God brings us each to himself in personal commitment, he joins us to the church and so brings us into a fellowship of people seeking to walk in his ways. It would be surprising if we could learn nothing from them.

All the contributors to this book have learned much from others. In fact, Lorimer Gray's chapter particularly emphasises this aspect of God's guidance through the various people God has brought into his life.

Many Christians (not all of them elderly) have lived for many years in fellowship with God and in obedience to his word and so have come to a practical understanding of his ways. Why not learn from their experience?

However, although treating their advice seriously, you should not view them as infallible. After all, although they may be able to identify with you quite deeply, this identification is never complete, and their understanding of your situation may therefore be partly defective. The better they know you and what you are facing, of course, the more helpful their advice is likely to be.

What about prophecy?

This, along with 'words of knowledge' and 'words of wisdom', is often said today to be a contemporary and not simply a Biblical phenomenon. Joel has had some experiences of this sort, and some of our other contributors have found Christians saying things to them quite strongly, because they were convinced they were meant to do so.

Perhaps the best approach to this question is that of writers who say that this phenomenon should not be regarded as something that has been in abeyance for centuries and has been renewed in recent decades. Many older Christians will recall how, in their earlier years, prior to the emergence of the charismatic movement and perhaps uninfluenced by Pentecostalism, they would be present in a group that was earnestly praying for guidance about some situation. After a time of prayer, one of the group would say something like this: 'God has given me a conviction that he wants us to do so and so.' Prophecy? Word of wisdom? Certainly it was not claimed to be such, but in content rather than form it often proved to be of the same order.

In such situations, the rest of the group would not always make an immediate response and accept the conviction of one as the guiding light for the group as a whole. Rather, if they were wise, they would test it by Scripture. So, in many Pentecostal and charismatic churches, in response to 1 Corinthians 14:29, words of 'prophecy', 'knowledge' and 'wisdom' are weighed carefully before they are accepted as God's truth.

If such words are placed on exactly the same level as Scripture, however, we really are in trouble!

The writer found a measure of reassurance a few years ago when he was present at a meeting where forty or fifty evangelical leaders of every brand were gathered. There were many Pentecostal and charismatic leaders among them. One of the speakers asked if any of them considered contemporary prophecy to be on the same level as Scripture and if so would they raise a hand. Not one of them did so.

It has to be acknowledged however that what responsible leaders may believe and what some on the fringe of a movement may practice, can be two quite different things.

As suggested in the Introduction, the advice of godly pastors ought to be of special value.

A pastor, by his calling, brings God's word to a congregation of God's people and he has a responsibility to God for those people. He has a special relationship therefore to the members of the local church and should be seeking God's face regularly for them.

It is wise and right therefore to pay special attention to those who, individually or collectively, have this kind of responsibility for you. Of course, it is important that they do not abuse their position and that their advice is always based on the great principles of Bible teaching.

Christian books too can play an important part in the story of our lives. If it were not so, then there would be no point in the writing and publishing of the present volume. Also the chapters you have read give a number of examples of guidance through literature. This is not surprising. God has given pastors and teachers to his church to upbuild it (Ephesians 4:11) and some of them have extended their spoken ministry by writing books.

Of course the writer of a book is one stage further removed from you than is a Christian friend. The element of personal acquaintance with you and your life is missing but it may be compensated for by another factor. You see, the writer of a book may give considerable thought to what he or she writes, and, if the writer is a Christian, will pray about it. So what has been written may at times have been be more carefully weighed than what is spoken, especially if the latter is somewhat 'off the cuff'.

Sometimes God may even use the spoken or written words of people who are not Christians. In many cases, godly wisdom and worldly wisdom are utterly different, poles apart. Paul makes this very clear in 1 Corinthians, chapters 1 to 4. His approving quotation of pagan poets from time to time, however, shows us that there are times when the two may coincide. We surely do not believe that every non-Christian is wrong all the time!

When we do think we discern the voice of God in the words of an unbeliever, however, we should take special care to weigh these words in the balance of Biblical truth.

The words even of Christian brothers and sisters need to be weighed in that balance too. The story is told that a wise old lay preacher was loaned a copy of a commentary by the author of it, who was a learned theologian. Some time later they met and the author asked the preacher how he was getting on with the commentary. 'Well, sir,' came the reply, 'I find that the

Scriptures throw a lot of light on it!'

It is not only through the words of Christian people that God guides us but through their lives. Every Christian should aim, by the grace of God, to be a role-model for those younger Christians who are within his or her sphere of influence. For a pastor this is quite indispensable. That Paul was able to say, 'Follow my example, as I follow the example of Christ' (1 Corinthians 11:1) presents a great challenge to those with pastoral responsibilities.

What about circumstances?

As Christians, we believe in the sovereignty of God over our lives, not only in large but also in small matters. This means we would expect his guidance through Scripture to cohere with the way he orders the practical circumstances of life. Donald found that an unexpected illness came at a time of important decision and played a part in it.

Circumstances may arise which call into question our concept of God's plan for us. It is foolish then to persist with the idea that we are being guided by God when our way is being blocked at every turn.

Or is it?

We must make an important distinction. At times God sovereignly uses adverse circumstances to test us. In such a situation, we need to realize that God's plan is that we should overcome these circumstances and not allow them to move us from the pathway of his will.

This means that we can never take circumstances as the sole guiding factor, particularly if they seem to be negative. There needs to be something else, some other

231

factor that God will bring into our situation to enable us to see whether to accept or to seek to overcome the things that are blocking the way.

So it is best for us to say that circumstances may furnish a general but not an infallible confirmation of God's guidance.

What about a personal invitation to engage in a particular piece of work or form of service?

Obviously this needs to be taken seriously. Barnabas was aware of a need at Antioch and he realized that Saul of Tarsus was well-fitted to meet that need, and so he invited him to join him in the work there. We do not know what thoughts this induced in the mind of Saul, but we do know that he accepted the invitation (Acts 11:25,26).

An invitation that comes from a group of godly people or even from a godly individual could well be a call from God. Such people will have prayed before making such an approach. They may in fact have been able to assess your suitability for the work in terms of gift, training and experience more fully than you yourself could do, because of the greater possibility of objectivity.

Such an invitation carries a large responsibility with it. You see, if you turn it down you make problems for those who have invited you. It means that they will begin to ask questions about their own sense of guidance.

Yet there are times when such invitations must be refused. It is essential, of course, for you to be fully persuaded in your own mind. The others concerned may have been able to assess your fitness for the work, but there could be others, perhaps many of them, who would also fit the bill. What is needed is not only fitness, important as that is, but a definite call from God. When all has been said, others cannot be guided or called for you.

Perhaps the best advice we can give is to treat the invitation as an important factor in guidance, but not as determining the issue without reference to other factors.

Of course, there are times when we are approached with a somewhat tentative suggestion rather than by a firm invitation. It would be wise to treat even this seriously as it may be God's will for us. Lorimer found that such a suggestion led to a long-term piece of service for him which was very much in line with his gifts, training, experience and personality.

What about the perception of a need you are able to fill?
I am not thinking about the small temporary need. Of course, if I am available and able to meet such a need, I hardly need much guidance about what to do. When it is a matter of a deep need which requires long-term or even lifelong commitment, then questions of guidance become very important.

When I was at college, we often debated the question, 'Does the need constitute the call?' As we had speakers representing different types of Christian work every single week, there could be no doubt that the answer must be either a negative or a seriously qualified positive. Obviously we could not respond to every need that was presented.

Some forms of service were automatically ruled out because we did not have the gifts or qualifications or training or experience, nor did there seem to be any possibility of making up these deficiencies. But still there were a great number of possible openings, each with its challenging need.

Again, the best advice is to take the need very seriously but not to let it be solely determinative. Who knows, perhaps you have been made aware of this need not so that you should go yourself (although you should be willing for this), but as a call for you to pray that God will send somebody. Maizie saw the need of children in Northern Ireland and became for a time occupied in helping to meet that need, and yet her discernment of the need in Brazil was really a call to pray rather than to go. Later the Lord called her to go out to Zaire.

What is true, of course, is that the God who knows the whole world will often move one of his servants from one place of service to another in order to meet a need. Sometimes the reason does not appear until later.

A fine missionary once wrote a letter in which she described herself as 'God's stop-gap', and this was right for her. Pauline has served the Lord in quite a number of countries, but always there have been factors that have made it clear that the change of location was in the plan of God. Mary too has had several moves, but is in no doubt that each has been intended by him. In fact such movement features in most of the stories told here.

The Saviour said to his disciples, 'The harvest is plentiful but the workers are few. Ask the Lord of the harvest, therefore, to send out workers into his harvest field' (Matthew 9:38). Be warned, though! Soon after he had thus called them to pray, he sent them into the harvest field (Matthew 10:1ff)!

2. Attitudes we should have
Some of these have already been stated or implied, but we now need to spell them out clearly.

We need to be receptive

This is where the Christian life begins. The parable of the sower (better called the parable of the soils) indicates both the primacy of the seed, which is the word, and also the vital importance of receptive soil, representing the human heart.

By nature, and because of our sinfulness, we are not like that. We are resistant to God and to his word. But God's amazing grace attunes our ears to hear his voice and opens our hearts to hear his word. This happens as, through the grace of the Holy Spirit, we are brought to the new birth and to faith in Christ.

This attitude needs to persist. 'If you hold to my teaching, you are really my disciples. Then you will know the truth, and the truth will set you free' (John 8:31,32), said our Lord. Much attention has been given to Paul's exhortation to be continually filled with the Spirit (Ephesians 5:18), but not enough to the companion exhortation (in a very similar context, as you will see if you examine them) to 'let the word of Christ dwell in you richly' (Colossians 3:16). We need to be like a river that is constantly renewed by waters coming down from its source in the hills.

Some of the contributors to this book have specially emphasized this. Read again the chapters by Donald and Mary in particular.

God guides us through other means than his word, although never in contradiction of it. It is wise then to accept his sovereignty over the whole of life and to be ready to hear his voice as it comes to us through the local church and its varied ministries, through Christian friends and through books.

Receptivity and expectancy go hand in hand. God has given so many promises of guidance that we should expect to receive it and be constantly sensitive to indications that he is speaking to us.

We need to be reflective

God has given us our minds and we should use them.

Christians often misunderstand the relationship between revelation and reason. They are not opposed to each other. What revelation seeks to counter is the worldly mind, not the mind as such, for it is God who has given us our mental powers. Paul says, 'we have the mind of Christ' (1 Corinthians 2:16) and 'be transformed by the renewing of your mind' (Romans 12:2).

There is a Christian mind. For every human being, thinking has to begin somewhere and with certain assumptions. The assumptions of the Christian mind are related to God's revelation in Scripture. We accept this by faith and then we go on to reason in a godly manner on the basis of it.

A striking example of this may be seen in the life of Abraham. We see in Genesis 22 that he was faced by what must have seemed an unbelievably irrational (as well as cruel) command by the God he loved. The Lord had made great promises to him and these promises were all focused on the son of his old age, Isaac. Now God was asking him to take Isaac to the place of sacrifice and offer him up as a burnt-offering. How incomprehensible! How agonizing!

Yet the Writer to the Hebrews has this to say, 'Abraham reasoned that God could raise the dead, and, figuratively speaking, he did receive Isaac back from death'

(Hebrews 11:19). Note the word 'reason'. This is a perfectly good translation of the Greek word used in this passage.

It seems as though Abraham's mind was active on the way from Beersheba to Moriah with his son. Probably he began to think about the promise of God and the command of God. How could they possibly be squared with each other? Then he may have begun to consider God's power. In so doing he was seeing something of the infinite resourcefulness and ability of God to fulfil his word of promise.

Why not follow Abraham's example? Reflect prayerfully on God's dealings with you. You may see a pattern in them. Think about your gifts and the way God has brought you, the providences of God in your life with him. A great modern evangelical preacher used to say that God usually guided him by showing him good reasons for doing things.

This does not mean that God will not do the unexpected. He is, in fact, very much the God of surprises. There are plenty of examples of that in the stories told here. But God's surprises always reflect his values, and, as we think about his dealings with us in the light of Scripture, we begin to see what those values are, and the fact that they provide the reasons for God's actions, which are therefore not arbitrary but are the expression of his perfect character.

We need to be reliant
That story of Abraham and Isaac illustrates this so well. As Hebrews says again, 'By faith Abraham, when God tested him, offered Isaac as a sacrifice' (Hebrews 11:17).

He knew that God was to be trusted. He had proved that to be true many times over. So when the big test came, he put his trust in God and set out to do his will.

Faith is the indispensable Christian virtue. Love may be greater but faith is even more fundamental, for it is out of faith that love and all other Christian virtues grow.

As each day comes, we recognize that we cannot predict what it will hold, but we place our hands in the hand of God so that we may move safely through the day.

Faith is often misunderstood. It is not 'a leap in the dark', but rather is response to light, the light of God's revelation of himself and his will. We see this as we examine the various Old Testament examples of faith recorded and commented on in Hebrews 11. So often, the faith of these people was a response to something God had said to them, in other words it was evoked by and moved into light that came from him.

We need to be ready
'Ready for all thy perfect will, mine acts of faith and love repeat ...'.

In some situations in which Christians find themselves, faith is undoubtedly the big issue. I am being asked to do something quite different from anything I have done before. Perhaps it involves giving up a well-paid and a secure job at a time of high unemployment. So the decision becomes a challenge to my faith.

Often, however, it is not faith that is the issue, but obedience, or perhaps faith and obedience together. God's work of grace in the heart of a Christian produces a new life, and we begin to want to do God's will because we are so grateful to him for his gift to us of Jesus Christ.

This is true in principle, but often in practice God's will encounters resistance in us.

Sometimes God faces us with the fact that some conduct or perhaps even the work we are doing is not fully consistent with the lifestyle of a Christian. In Paul Harvey's case it meant leaving a job.

We know that God's will is really best, and yet we still want our own way. Pauline found a need to surrender to God in the areas of marriage, money and career. Maizie has told us so honestly how she tried on several occasions to bargain with God, but how God had his way with her.

We know there is treasure in heaven for us, and yet we make a good bank balance a major concern of life. We know that Jesus made himself of no reputation, and yet we enjoy the praise of others. We know that he has called all his disciples to deny themselves, take up the cross and follow him, and yet we still pamper ourselves and seek lives of ease.

What is the cure for this? Is it to read the lives of Christians who found that rebellion against God did not pay, or to think about sadly backslidden believers you know and the shipwreck they have made of their lives? Perhaps this may help a little, but there is a better way.

It is to spend time at the cross. Read the accounts of the passion and death of Jesus. Remember that it was for you he endured such agony. Think of what life and eternity would be like without him and his dying love.

Obedience that is only a matter of expediency is still linked to a motive that is less than the best. True and deep obedience is grounded in profound gratitude to a wonderfully gracious and loving Saviour. This is the obedience that is undergirded by the Spirit of God.

Wondering what God wants you to do and how you can be sure of his will? Be receptive; be open to his word! Be reflective; use the mind he has given you to apply his word to your own situation! Be reliant; wait on him for guidance and trust yourself to him! Be ready to walk in his ways. They are the best ways, and surely obedience is the only response you can make to his great love!